A
PEAKLAND
ABECEDARY

JULIE BUNTING

ISBN 0-901100-82-X

Designed and Printed by
Northend Creative Print Solutions,
Sheffield S8 0TZ

Tel: 0114 250 0331 Fax: 0114 250 0676
Email: ks@northend.co.uk

ACHERS & ACRES

The Church of All Saints in Bakewell has a wealth of fine ecclesiastical work, in particular some imaginative oak carving. Winged dragons, mythical beasts and a mermaid appear on the misericords of the choir stalls, where a witty pictorial pun is revealed beneath the priest's seat. Here the relief of a grotesque cross-eyed head accompanies a cow beneath three rotten teeth. The scene is a representation of the Biblical 'one cow to three acres' — the troublesome molars being the 'achers'. Other strange figures are carved between the misericords; one of the quaintest is a chubby contorted tumbler caught in the middle of a backward somersault. His face peers from between his pointed boots as he slides downwards, head first.

AQUEDUCT

An odd little aqueduct over Mill Lane at Cromford has been conspicuous by its absence since it was demolished by a passing lorry in late 2002. Yet its restoration is certain, for this is an important industrial relic connected with Arkwright's Cromford Mill. Unlike the great stone aqueducts which carry Cromford Canal over the rivers Derwent and Amber a short distance away, this modest iron structure of 1821 was built to carry the waters of Cromford Sough (*see Bear Pit*), via the outflow from Scarthin pond, across to waterwheels that powered the cotton mill. An abundant water supply was the essential factor in Arkwright's choice of site for what was to become the world's first successful water-powered cotton mill.

ARBOR LOW

Arbor Low is the most important prehistoric monument in the north of England, standing at 1,230 ft on an exposed limestone plateau in the White Peak. Sometimes known as the Stonehenge of the North, it comprises an earthen henge (bank) of approximately 290 ft diameter and an internal ditch with two entrances into the central area, where some 50 recumbent limestone slabs centre on a small arrangement of stones known as a cove.

Arbor Low is of late Neolithic or early Bronze Age construction, around 2000 BC. The height from the top of the bank to the bottom of the ditch, around 12 ft now, was originally about 18 ft. Only one of the stones is semi-upright and archaeological opinion is divided as to whether they were originally placed in a prone or an upright position.

A low ditch and bank leads from the henge in the direction of Gib Hill tumulus, 350 yards away. For all the archaeological study of this impressive monument, the mystery of Arbor Low lies in its origins and a knowledge that died with our early ancestors. If the circle had a religious purpose, it may not be too fanciful to imagine a certain atmosphere there still, whatever one's beliefs.

ASH HOUSE

A small, round stone building in a field alongside a lane between Hassop and Baslow is known locally as the ash house. It was once a store place for blocks of potash, prepared nearby and sent away for use in glass making. One old tale refers to the hut as the sometime home of a shepherd, who hid his meagre savings between slabs in the stone roof. A thief got to hear of this but when he climbed onto the roof slabs they gave way, killing him, the shepherd and his dog. Legend has it that the sound of the shepherd whistling his dog can still occasionally be heard on the surrounding hills.

ASHFORD MARBLE

Today Ashford in the Water slumbers undisturbed by the demands of industry but was once the centre of a craft spanning three centuries. A dark, fine-grained limestone which occurs to the west of Ashford takes on a jet black gloss when polished. As early as 1580, Bess of Hardwick, always loyal to local products, used Ashford marble for the chimney piece of the great High Presence Chamber at Hardwick Hall.

Quarries were gradually opened up to meet a growing demand for this ornamental stone and in 1748 Henry Watson built England's first water-powered marble mill on the Wye at Ashford. Local varieties of limestone and fluorspar were used for coloured inlay work, a painstaking skill diverted into a cottage industry that turned out tables, pedestals, vases and ornaments *(see Underground Riches)*. At the Great Exhibition of 1851, the quality and beauty of Ashford marble put even prestigious Italian workmanship in the shade. Trinkets and jewellery, paperweights and snuff boxes, crosses, obelisks and barometers were soon widely on sale.

Ashford marble mill closed in 1905. Examples of local output have become increasingly prized; the bowl illustrated here is part of a beautiful collection in Buxton Museum & Art Gallery. Ashford parish church displays a prize-winning table of 1882 as a reminder of a time when local skills carried the name of Ashford Marble around Britain and beyond.

BEAR PIT

Older residents of Cromford have little truck with this nickname for a feature that they say 'was never known as *that* when we were young'. Bears have nothing to do with this walled, open pit hidden away at the lower end of Cromford Hill. The water reaching daylight at the bottom of the shaft is the tail of Cromford Sough, driven over 320 years ago to drain lead mines, a major undertaking further extended in the 18th century. The pit was constructed in 1785 to give access to sluice machinery, still in situ, which regulated the flow of water from the sough. The output was put to good use at Richard Arkwright's cotton mill but nowadays continues unhindered to feed

Cromford Canal. The 'bear pit' lies down an alleyway opposite the road junction to Bonsall, a short distance above Cromford market place.

BEE BOLES

Once upon a distant time, Britain was known as 'An Isle of Honey'. In the Anglo-Saxon period, honey was one of the resources accepted as manorial dues from manors including Darley, Matlock, Wirksworth, Ashbourne, Parwich, Hope, Ashford and Bakewell. Over the centuries,

beekeepers have housed their busy little workers in hollowed logs, tubular clay vessels and straw domes called skeps. Skeps were often protected from the weather inside bee boles or bee garths — deep recesses built into garden walls.

Bee boles in stone country are believed to date from the 17th century. A row of about ten boles can be seen at the base of a crumbling gritstone wall near Cuckoostone quarry on Matlock Moor. Rather formal later examples are kept in good order at the former Milford Hotel in Bakewell, as well as several older boles in a nearby private garden. Also on private sites are a single 'bee niche' in a limestone rockface at Miller's Dale, a row at Goatsciffe and a superb sequence on a farm near Wingerworth. Others, now blocked in, include a group at Robin Hood near Baslow and a single example at Beeley.

BLUE JOHN

This famous mineral is a type of fluorite that occurs in 14 named banding patterns at Castleton. The Blue John Cavern retains small deposits of the mineral, which since 1750 has also been mined in Treak Cliff Cavern. Here is the largest remaining single known piece of Blue John, a 6 ft-thick pillar

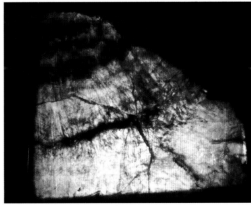

weighing about 15 tons. Only jewellery and small trinkets can now be manufactured from the diminished deposits but magnificent ornamental and inlay work — often carefully illuminated to reveal the translucent bands of purple, blue and yellow — is displayed in many of our stately homes, along with an impressive collection in Buxton Museum and Art Gallery. Shown here is a lovely sample displayed in Castleton Information Centre.

BONSALL CROSS

No document proving Bonsall's right to hold a regular market has ever come to light, in fact an application for a market charter in the late 1600s is known to have been refused. Nevertheless, a tall stone cross on a flight of circular steps occupies prime position in the village centre. The cross shaft may date to the 15th or even 14th century and in 1678 was topped with a gritstone ball bearing carved faces. The shaft was restored in the 1870s at the expense of a member of the wealthy Prince family of Bonsall *(see Marble Bridges)*. Old photographs show the ball topped with an ornate metal rod but this was taken down for repair about 30 years ago and never replaced.

BRIDGE CHAPEL

On the downstream side of Cromford Bridge are the remains of a small, perhaps 15th century bridge chapel, one of very few left in England. When the chapel was built beside a probable narrow timber bridge, travellers had good reason to give thanks for their safe arrival here and to pray for an uneventful continuation of their journey. A guiding lantern may have shone through the small round window which still peeps over the River Derwent and can be seen here through the old arched doorway.

Alison Uttley, recounting old tales of her native Cromford, dreamt up a monk who lived in the chapel and helped travellers to ford the perilous river. By the 16th century, the building was in use as a parochial chapelry of Wirksworth but by the mid-1600s was no longer used as a place of worship. A restoration of the tumbledown remains was carried out in 1952. A few mossy steps lie between the outer walls, while turf-covered mounds indicate where the foundations extended 30 ft along the river bank.

BUBBLING SPRINGS

After periods of rain, the headwaters of the lovely River Lathkill issue from a source inside Lathkill Head Cave. In the dry days of summer, though, they emerge lower down the valley, gurgling to the surface from subterranean 'bubbling springs'. Impassive frogs thrive in the gentle movement of these clearest of waters, noted for their abundance of fish and insect life. From Conksbury Bridge, a pretty walk follows the river upstream through Lathkill Dale, passing its many sparkling weirs before reaching Lathkill Head Cave and continuing towards Monyash.

BUCK STONE

Lying amongst the bracken below Stanage Edge is a large gritstone boulder known as the Buck Stone. Its name is perhaps derived from 'bucket', since a nearby spring may have served as a watering place for travellers and their horses. The spot lies on an ancient packhorse route from Sheffield via Stanedge Pole to Hathersage. (For some reason, the Pole is spelt differently from the Edge.)

About two centuries ago, a simple dwelling was constructed against the Buck Stone, utilising its sides as interior walls. The adjoining ground was levelled to take lean-to structures, with socket holes bored into the stone for rafters and supports. Rainwater grooves were cut into the upper surface of the stone and down the rock face. Apparently of the same age is the carving of a 'pin man'. His fingers and triangular head, along with a roughly rounded object by his side, are formed by 'pecked' holes. Few people discover this strange figure by chance and its original purpose seems purely decorative.

BULL RINGS

Bull baiting was common throughout England for hundreds of years, not only as entertainment but because it was believed to tenderise the meat. Chained to a thick metal ring, the bull was tormented by dogs specially trained to pin him by the nose — the one area which really was tender. Every market town and many villages had a bull

Bridge Chapel

ring, of which only a handful survive around the Peak. The Foolow ring is still embedded in a large boulder by the village cross, whilst that of Eyam is preserved in The Square. At Snitterton, near Matlock, a bull ring survives in its original road-level position near the junction of a secluded lane and the road through the village. Bonsall bull ring, pictured here, has been kept inside the parish church since around 1834, when the kind-hearted vicar purchased a bull from its large crowd of tormentors at the village wakes, bulldogs straining at the leash. Bull baiting was banned by law the following year.

CANNON BOLLARDS

Though they scarcely get a second look, cast-iron bollards are familiar items of street furniture, generally tapering from a broad base to a spherical tip. Manufactured in various sizes over a long period, these are known as cannon bollards. The design was born in the 18th century, when a new use was found for the barrels of redundant cannons.

Some original cannon bollards can be seen at Cromford; the most obvious stands on the pavement outside Arkwright's Mill. They originate from a time when the mill was armed against possible attack during the Luddite riots, with advances in hosiery manufacture putting home-based framework knitters out of work. Rioters destroyed Arkwright's Chorley mill in 1779

and he subsequently equipped his Cromford factory with 'Fifteen hundred Stand of small Arms ... a great Battery of Cannon' and 'upwards of five hundred Spears ... fixt in Poles of between 2 and 3 Yards long.' The threat never materialised and at least three of his cannon survive as bollards, their muzzles set with authentic iron cannon balls.

CARL WARK

Visible from many miles around, the moorland promontory of Higger Tor, east of Hathersage, has on its slopes a two-acre plateau, buttressed by what appears from a distance to be a lengthy outcrop of gritstone. This is Carl Wark, a largely natural defensive fortress in high isolation 1,250 ft above sea level. It was probably during the Iron Age that the site was strengthened with earthen ramparts and countless tons of unhewn boulders, some as long as 10 feet and 3 feet thick. This defensive work is evident on the western side, the most vulnerable section had it come under attack. A Scheduled Ancient Monument, Carl Wark lies on access land and can be reached by various footpaths.

CELTIC HERITAGE

Our Celtic ancestors left us with Peakland place-names, folklore and links to earth worship in such traditions as Castleton Garland and our famous well dressings. A Celtic giant named Aigle takes credit for hurling the massive Eagle Stone into position on Baslow Edge. Another of his tribe, the giant Hulac Warren, was himself transformed into a large rock in the River Wye near Monsal Dale. This is his eternal punishment for trying to ravish a beautiful shepherdess named Hedessa, who died protecting her virtue.

A smattering of tangible Celtic relics survive in ancient stone carvings brought under the wing of the Church *(see Sheela-na-Gig)*. Brassington church contains a crudely hewn stone head, similar to others displayed in local museums or preserved semi-secretly in stone walls around the Peak.

CHRISOM

A chrisom was a white linen cloth formerly laid on newly baptised infants following anointment with the holy oil or chrism, as set out in the first Prayer Book of Edward VI (1549): 'Then the Godfathers and Godmothers shall take and lay their hands upon the child, and the minister shall put upon him his white vesture, commonly called the chrisom ...' The cloth was worn for seven days and then returned to the church, though if the infant died within that time the chrisom became its shroud, bound with ornamental folds or strips of linen. This practice is demonstrated in Bakewell parish church, where the rare effigy of a tightly swathed baby stands on a 17th-century monument to Sir George Manners and his wife, Grace Pierpont. The child was their first-born son who died in infancy and is shown beneath his parents as a sorrowful little figure amongst the effigies of his surviving siblings, including the brother who was to become heir in his stead.

CLAPPER BRIDGES

The Peak has a wealth of picturesque stone bridges, straddling waters crossed by ancient highways and byways. Those which reveal themselves only to foot travellers include sturdy, age-old clapper bridges. Supported on piles of stones sunk into the river bed, the span simply consists of a

massive stone slab or two. A clapper bridge with two 9 ft slabs, inscribed with the dates 1742 and 1777, crosses the Bar Brook west of the A621, north of Baslow. Another example fords the Rymas Brook between Hassop and Pilsley but one of the busiest, and most photogenic, lies on the Limestone Way crossing of the River Bradford below Holywell Lane in Youlgrave. Longer than all of these put together is this multi-slab clapper bridge that carries a footpath over the River Amber, south of Ashover.

COFFIN PATHS

Occasionally known as corpse roads, these are exactly what they say. Their sombre names rarely appear on maps but most are still in use as footpaths, always heading in the direction of a church. Their origins date to a time when only the well-to-do made their final journey on a horse-drawn hearse. Otherwise the deceased was borne on the shoulders of relatives and friends.

Memories from Winster tell that when a coffin was due to be carried along the main street, people would leave chairs outside their houses for the bearers to stop awhile. Some country parishes were so extensive that coffins had to be carried for several miles, so difficult sections of the route came to be paved. One such coffin path descends the steep hilly fields below Overton, in use at a time when Ashover parish extended in this direction as far as Lea and Tansley.

CONVEX WEIR

A rare example of a convex weir spans the Derwent in Matlock Bath, just upstream of Masson Mills. Its distinctive shape, an exact reverse of the familiar concave design, was dictated by a natural curve of the underwater rocks. Water from the weir was directed into a fast-running channel to power the machinery of the cotton mill, established by Arkwright in 1783.

Around 50 years later, a writer named William Adam visited Matlock Bath. Greatly impressed by Masson Mill and its scenic surroundings, he described entering the dale from Cromford, with a sudden turn in the road 'disclosing at once the splendid rocks which burst upon the view through a fine opening up the river, exhibiting a beautiful waterfall, foaming over the "weir" and rough bed below it ...'

Masson Mills were in continuous use until 1991 and now house a working textile museum with views towards the back-to-front weir.

CRINKLE CRANKLE WALL

This is the wonderfully descriptive name for a high, red brick roadside wall on the north side of Hopton Hall near Wirksworth. The sinuous design dates from the mid-18th century in England and was not merely an ornamental whim, since the curved lines give added strength without the need for buttressing. Such walls generally served for growing fruit, their inner bays trapping warmth from the sun as well as providing shelter from wind and frost.

Derbyshire has another crinkle crankle wall in the garden of the primary school at

Sudbury and another at Eggington, where it forms the boundary between the churchyard and old rectory. Claimant for the longest example in the world is a red brick wall encircling the village of Easton in Suffolk. As an architectural style the feature is also known as a ribbon or serpentine wall, and it is easy to see why the Hopton wall is credited for inspiring the planting of a serpentine beech hedge at Chatsworth in 1953.

DAMBUSTERS

The Derwent and Howden reservoirs, in the Upper Derwent Valley, are a major link in the water supply chain feeding the Peak District and surrounding counties. The reservoirs played a national role during the Second World War, when RAF bomber pilots used them as stand-ins for the Ruhr dams of industrial Germany. The pilots were practising for the epic raids of May 1943, when the Möhne and Eder dams were breached by the purposely invented 'bouncing bombs'.

A memorial near the reservoir commemorates the legendary 617 'Dambuster' Squadron, who wittily adopted as their motto 'Après moi le deluge'. A museum in the west tower of Derwent Dam, open most Sundays, is dedicated to the Squadron and its famous raid. Bombers again flew over Derwent dams during the 1954 filming of The Dambusters.

DAYKIN

Beloved of naturalists and water life, the crystal rivers Lathkill and Bradford flow through lovely limestone dales to unite at Alport, near Youlgrave. Their confluence marks the beginning of a two-mile stretch of water, the River Daykin — a name lost to memory until rediscovered in the early 1970s by writer W.H. Brighouse. Almost at the start of its journey, the Daykin was formerly put to work at the wheel of Alport

corn mill. The river still glides past the old mill, tumbling over a weir en route for a leisurely journey to join the Wye below Congreave bridge.

DEVIL'S ARSE

It might have been thought a brave move to thus rename Peak Cavern at Castleton in recent years, if not downright rude. Yet the place was unashamedly called the Devil's Arse for centuries, when the 'a' word was considered not at all vulgar and freely used by early travel writers. An explanation of the name arises from a legend that the cavern is one of the entrances to Hell. In 1621, Ben Jonson penned a ballad wherein the Devil himself was dined in the cavern by the Prince of Thieves, feasting on such dainties as 'A rich fat Usurer stewed in his marrow'. It was in the 17th century that Thomas Hobbes included the Devil's Arse amongst his Seven Wonders of the Peak, assuring its future as a major tourist attraction. Added interest comes from the relics of a ropemaking industry that thrived inside the cavern for many generations *(see Ropeworks)*.

DEWPONDS & MERES

Although the preference tends towards meres, either of these words can refer to the circular ponds that store rainwater in limestone areas of the Peak. Mere-builders worked to traditional skills, first excavating a circular hollow with sloping sides that would make the water easily accessible to cattle and sheep. The hollow was lined with slaked lime several inches thick, forming an impenetrable barrier to earthworms, which would wreck the whole enterprise if they burrowed through the subsequent layer of clay. The prepared clay was slapped hard against the base and sides of the basin, working upwards towards ground level, with even the tiniest joint thoroughly beaten out. Next, the clay was covered with a layer of gravel or ashes and pitched with stone. Finally, the wide rim was strengthened with stone and gravel.

An old misconception about the term 'dew ponds' needs to be laid to rest: they are not topped up by morning dew but take their name from an 18th century pond-maker named Dew.

DOGWHIP

Dogwhips are a thankfully rare commodity but one very mean-looking specimen, with a leather-bound handle and hide thong, is on view inside Baslow parish church. Between the 16th and 19th centuries, numerous English churches employed an official dog whipper to keep order during divine

service. The wonderfully gossipy parish accounts of Youlgrave complain about having to pay their dog whipper a whole year's salary in a single instalment in 1759 — 'a hardship to the Parish for want of ... keeping a proper date in there [sic] accounts'. But whether breaking up fights between dogs taken into church by their owners — the usual story — or grabbing unaccompanied canines which sneaked inside during prayers, a whip-wielding official can only have added to the distraction.

DRY STONE WALLS

Dry stone walls are by no means exclusive to the Peak District but our plentiful supplies of fossil-laden limestone and darker gritstone provide the material for thousands of miles of boundary walls. Irregular stretches may have their origins in delineating early homesteads and common land, though most patterns were laid out some two centuries ago under land enclosures. Dry stone walls define boundaries, provide shelter for livestock and just as usefully have been the means of clearing stone-littered fields for grazing or the plough.

An experienced waller can build 15 to 20 feet in a day. His tools are few; stringlines and a wooden frame guide the tapering wall upwards from its broad base, with intermittent full-width anchorage stones called 'throughs' and ending with a vertical top row of 'copers'. Each stone is held in place only by skilled positioning but the finished work should need little maintenance for at least the first quarter-century of its long life.

DUKE'S BIRDCAGES

The existence of these upmarket 'birdcages' was a bit of a secret in their day. Each was a love nest for one or other of the mistresses of William Spencer Cavendish, 6th Duke of Devonshire (1790-1858), son of the celebrated Georgiana.

Devonshire had been forced to become more circumspect after pursuing romance on the London scene, only to find himself named in the memoirs of a celebrated

courtesan. So he set up favourite paramours in various houses on his Chatsworth estate, including Calton House, Heathy Lea, Dunsa House and The Rookery at Ashford *(pictured)*. It may have been the name of The Rookery which inspired the local nickname 'birdcages', for it was here that Devonshire installed Elizabeth Warwick, his mistress for ten years from 1827. His diary of 1828 tells of his 'unalloyed happiness with Elizabeth' even though he is soon confessing to thoughts of others. William Spencer Cavendish never did lose his heart to a suitable bride but is known to history as The Bachelor Duke.

EAGLE STONE

This massive natural boulder on the moorland above Baslow Edge may take its name from Aigle, a Celtic deity with a penchant for hurling enormous rocks around the countryside. Our pagan ancestors seem to have held Aigle responsible for lobbing this one up here. Generations of young Baslow men used to face a different sort of challenge when, in compliance with local custom, they had to scale the Eagle Stone to prove their readiness for marriage. For those in the know and in spite of its forbidding profile, there is a relatively easy route to the summit.

EARL GREY TOWER

The Thornhills of Stanton Hall erected this square gritstone tower on Stanton Moor to commemorate a true politician of the people. As Whig Prime Minister, Charles, second Earl Grey, introduced the 1832 Reform Bill which brought 'people power' to Parliament and set the foundation for universal suffrage. A wealthy minority, represented by the House of Lords, had fought tooth and nail to retain their exclusive voting rights but Grey persevered and his bill was passed at the third attempt. It earned him the gratitude of a nation half-starved and on the verge of revolt. Now missing from the tower is an inscribed stone bearing a coronet and the words 'Earl Grey 1832'.

EBBING & FLOWING WELLS

Famed as one of the Wonders of the Peak in a 17th century poem by Thomas Hobbes, tutor to the young Cavendishes at Chatsworth, an ebbing and flowing phenomenon became essential viewing for the 18th century travellers who braved the wild Peak as our earliest tourists.

In fact, two places laid claim to wells which were believed to rise and fall with the tide. One was at Tideswell and the other at Barmoor Clough, where a spring still feeds a semi-circular chain of troughs in a grassy hollow beside the A623. Many passers-by have witnessed the siphonic action of this capricious spring, which supposedly rose at over 1,000 gallons a minute to fill the depression with a pond 12 ft across and 2/3 ft deep. The water would then ebb steadily away through drainage outlets, the entire performance all over inside ten minutes and not reported now for many years.

ECTON COPPER MINES

Traces of surface buildings and disused shafts stand as visible evidence of copper mining on Ecton Hill, in the Manifold Valley, worked from the Bronze Age into the late 19th century. Records were broken at Ecton: in 1670 here was the first British mine to use gunpowder and by the following century its principal shaft, at

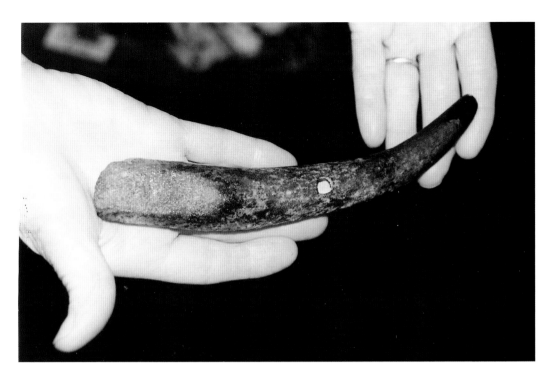

1,400 ft, was the deepest ever sunk in Britain. Boats provided haulage along the subterranean streams and the 300-strong workforce included women ore-breakers and child sorters as young as eight. Tradition has it that just one year's revenue enabled the Duke of Devonshire, owner of the mines, to build the magnificent Buxton Crescent. An antler pick recovered from Ecton workings has been radiocarbon dated to the Bronze Age.

ELEPHANT ON A WALL

This quirky relief of a black elephant is fixed to the rear wall of a mock-Tudor building at Park Head in Matlock. Its

existence dates from the days when the premises were Burgon's High Class Grocery and Provisions stores; their Namunah trademark carried the logo of an elephant. The tusker, with the word Namunah on its flanks, is easily seen from the clock tower area in Hall Leys Park.

EMPEROR FOUNTAIN

Viewed through its own rainbow on a sunny day, the Emperor Fountain is the pride of Chatsworth's water features. Designed by Joseph Paxton, it was constructed in 1843 as an impressive showpiece for the intended visit of Tsar Nicholas of All the Russias, who unfortunately did not turn up. The fountain is gravity fed and capable of a 298 ft jet, which lowers an eight-acre lake above the house by four inches an hour. Although not continuously seen at full play, the Emperor Fountain currently performs its spectacular displays on summer afternoons and special occasions.

EVERLASTING WREATH

A wreath of everlasting flowers in St Peter's church at Edensor was a personal tribute from Queen Victoria on the death of Lord Frederick Cavendish, second son of the 7th Duke of Devonshire. As Chief Secretary for Ireland, Lord Frederick was sent to Dublin in May 1882 with a message of peace from Prime Minister Gladstone. Within hours of his arrival, Cavendish was stabbed to death

in Phoenix Park. His body was brought back to Edensor for burial and over a quarter of a million mourners lined the route taken by the cortège through Chatsworth Park. The Duke of Devonshire was devastated by the murder of his 'beloved Freddie' and never recovered from the loss.

EWE TURNS

Sheep are not best known for their homing instincts but thereby hangs a tale, or rather two tails and two handsome heads. In 1830, two Woodland sheep managed to confound the entire farming community in

Hope and for miles around. They had been sent to auction from Rowlee Farm and the successful bidder took them to pastures new in Kent, from where the homesick pair soon went missing. They somehow managed to walk more than 200 miles in the right direction to reach their familiar High Peak moors. Nobody seems to have asked what their rightful owner had to say but the Rowlee farmer was sympathetic to his prodigal sheep and allowed them to live out their natural lives in the place they loved best. When they died, their heads were mounted and hung in Hope church but can now be seen in Buxton Museum & Art Gallery.

FAIR FLORA

Above the road between Grindleford and Eyam is privately owned Stoke Wood, where on a pedestal in a high clearing stands Fair Flora, a stone statue garlanded in blossoms. Many mysterious happenings brought Flora to this sylvan spot. Her

FISHBELLY RAIL

This type of cast-iron rail was used in the early days of Cromford & High Peak Railway. It takes its name from the curved flange which gives strength along its central section; the ends were supported on stone blocks rather than wooden sleepers. Lengths of fishbelly rail can be seen in situ at High Peak Junction Workshops and built into a plinth beside the High Peak Trail near Middleton Top.

FISHING TEMPLES

The River Dove was the inspiration for Izaak Walton, whose classic work *The Compleat Angler* was published in 1653 *(see Viator's Bridge)*. Nearly 20 years later, his angling companion and formally adopted son, Charles Cotton, built a fishing temple for their exclusive use in Beresford Dale. Walton was already in his 80th year but for a further decade he and Cotton often stayed at this small stone lodge. Its one room is 15 ft square with a fireplace and pretty latticed windows beneath a stone slate roof. The entwined initials of Walton and Cotton are inscribed over the doorway with the words 'Piscatoribus Sacrum'. The building stands on private land but is visible from a path on the opposite bank.

original home may have been Chatsworth before she was given to Stoke Hall. With her arrival, though, came ill-fortune and supposed hauntings, so her new family banished her to the woods. Another local tradition claims that the statue is a memorial to a daughter of Stoke Hall, who drowned after slipping from the stepping stones on the Derwent while eloping with her lover.

When Flora made a television appearance in 2006, expert opinion attributed the workmanship to William John Coffee (1774 -1846), a modeller for Crown Derby porcelain and internationally renowned sculptor of larger works. The owner of Stoke Hall Quarry kindly allows Flora to receive visitors during reasonable hours, since there is no public right of way.

The same motto, meaning 'sacred to fishermen', is carved above the door of an 18th century fishing lodge at Cromford Bridge on the Derwent. This little building was once home to Sir Richard Arkwright's water bailiff and remained in occupation until 1914. The remains of an adjoining medieval bridge chapel were used as an outhouse *(see Bridge Chapel)*.

FOLLIES

Built as labours of love or eccentric whims of the wealthy, true follies are rather rare in the Peak. Yet in the late 17th century, a local clergyman carved shelters, steps and armchairs into Rowtor Rocks *(qv)*, where he spent his free time admiring the surrounding scenery. Unknown hands sculpted a number of stone boulders on the summit of Harborough Rocks near Brassington, roughly hewn into a huge chair, a font and a pulpit, all as proudly useless as a folly should be.

A few frivolities were built at the expense of good-hearted landowners to provide employment when jobs were scarce. They

include Boot's Folly — a stone tower erected on Bradfield Moor in 1927, Solomon's Temple on Grin Low at Buxton, and the Prospect or Victoria Tower on the Heights of Abraham at Matlock Bath. On the opposite hillside stands Riber Castle, built in 1862 and mocked as Smedley's Folly when its designer and owner, the hydropathic pioneer John Smedley, struggled to obtain a reliable water supply.

An improved water supply in the 1870s is the story behind Cross's Folly, an ornate stone water fountain near Bakewell bridge *(pictured)*. Robert Cross of Milford House instigated its construction to mark the new undertaking but not all the townspeople were happy about abandoning their free pumps and wells in return for a system linked to a water rate.

FONTS, PEA SOUP & BULLETS

The oldest feature in an English church may be its font. Early, simple stone tubs are found in Peakland churches including Eyam, Darley Dale and Tissington. Many fonts were confiscated during the Commonwealth along with other church valuables, though a few were hidden until safer times. Some of these lay forgotten for several centuries. The Norman font now in Youlgrave church was retrieved from the garden of Elton vicarage 160 years ago. A side stoup for holy water or oil makes it unique in all England. Tideswell parish font was rescued from a rubbish heap in the 18th century after serving as a paint vessel, while that of Taddington was discovered in Victorian times in the kitchen of a nearby inn, only recently emptied of pea soup though normally used for washing beer glasses.

Ashover font, pictured here, is a great rarity for its lead bowl; it narrowly escaped being melted down into bullets when Roundhead soldiers over-ran the village in 1646. The importance of our ancient fonts has become far more appreciated in modern times. When Derwent church was 'drowned' by a reservoir in the 1940s, the font which had served its parishioners for three centuries was given an appreciative new home in the Church of the Holy Trinity, Tansley.

FRAMEWORK KNITTERS' WORKSHOPS

The production of silk stockings became a well established cottage industry after the invention of the stocking frame around 1590. These hand looms kept entire families in employment in their own homes, even after the factory system was introduced during the Industrial Revolution.

Here in the Peak, framework knitting thrived at Bonsall over many generations. A well-lit workshop with a datestone of 1737 survives in Bonsall Dale, where William Oliver worked as a silk knitter all his life, operating up to 24 frames. William died in 1872 and his workshop was reopened by his daughter, who with at least three other Bonsall stockingers became outworkers for I. & R. Morley of Nottingham. A larger, 19th century workshop stands just above Bonsall Cross, one of the last to remain in use into the past century.

A stockingers' shop can also be seen on Royal Oak Terrace at Crich, complete with its expanse of upper windows. These typical long windows were essential to the intricate work carried out inside.

FROG STONE

Built into a wall at Mottram Cutting, this curiosity is photographed here by Neville T. Sharpe, who tells its story in *The Land of the Etherow*. Inevitably known as the frog stone, it seems to bear out unlikely tales of living amphibians found encased in stone. As Neville relates: 'At the International Exhibition in London in 1862 a piece of coal with the shape of a frog in it was on show together with a live frog which was claimed to have been discovered inside.'

Our frog stone dates from the construction of Mottram Cutting in the early 19th century, when one of the workmen split open a piece of rock and out jumped a frog or toad. It left a clear imprint in the solid stone and although quite weathered now, the outline is still evident against a background coat of whitewash.

FULWOOD'S ROCK

In the autumn of 1643, with England rent by civil war, 1,100 Derbyshire men, mainly lead miners, were mustered by Sir Christopher Fulwood of Fulwood Castle at Middleton by Youlgrave, to fight for Charles 1. When this alarming news reached Parliamentarian leader Sir John Gell, he despatched a company of Roundheads to

Middleton. Fulwood fled but was cornered behind a rocky fissure at the head of Bradford Dale. He was taken prisoner with wounds that proved fatal.

Fulwood Castle fell into disuse for about 80 years and was then demolished; the stone was reused in building Castle Farm close by. Grassy mounds behind the farm hide traces of limestone walls and foundations, the last remnants of 'an embattled house of great magnitude.' Down by the River Bradford, Fulwood's Rock bears evidence of the spot where a desperate young Royalist made his last stand.

GARDEROBES

In 1176, a huge square keep was constructed for William Peveril's castle at Castleton *(qv)*, its two storeys contained within 8 ft-thick outer walls. A winding passage in the south-east wall of the upper floor still leads to a garderobe, the oldest

indoor privy in the Peak. Its position is revealed from outside by one small window *(pictured)*. The outlet from the privy was simply an open-ended chute built within the thickness of the wall to discharge its contents at ground level. Garderobes in larger castles were commonly built one above the other on different floors but sharing the same chute — which emptied into the moat, where there was one. Recent conservation by English Heritage has opened up visitor access to two previously inaccessible chambers at Peak Castle, including the garderobe.

An indoor privy was quite a status symbol, as would have been the case with a Tudor garderobe still in situ at Bakewell Old House Museum. It dates back at least 500 years, discreetly tucked away in a windowless cubby hole above a 9 ft shaft that emerges at the foot of what was originally an outer wall.

GARLAND

The colourful Castleton Garland tradition has probable origins in an age-old fertility rite. It takes place on 29 May, Oak Apple Day, the date on which Charles 11 escaped Parliamentary soldiers by hiding in an oak tree. Maypole dancing plays a part in Castleton Garland celebrations but the central character is the King, dressed in Stuart costume though barely visible beneath the enormous floral Garland, heavy with blossom and greenery, covering his head and shoulders. Accompanied by his consort, a procession and band, the King tours the village on horseback before being relieved of the Garland, which is hoisted to the top of St Edmund's church tower and left to wither.

Changing displays of early Garland memorabilia are on show in Castleton Information Centre.

GENNELS & JITTIES

... otherwise known as jennels, ginnels, guinnels, gunnels or perhaps jitties — all spoken with a soft 'j'. Depending on the locality, these words all describe a narrow alleyway between buildings and generally passable only on foot. The alley might also be called a twitchet or perhaps an entry.

Here in the Peak, gennel is the favoured word in old stone villages such as Winster, Longnor, Youlgrave and Matlock Bath. An entry, on the other hand, often refers to a covered passage giving access to the rear of houses on either side. Some entries run beneath an overhanging bedroom belonging to one or other of the properties. For some readers, this type of passage would be a jitty!

GREAT BARMOTE COURT

The rights and customs of lead mining were already ancient when they gained legal recognition at the Inquisition for the King's Field of the High Peak, held at Ashbourne in 1288. Lead mining laws were henceforth to be enforced by Great Barmote Courts, two of which still sit on a regular basis. Eyam hosts the annual Barmote Court of the Joint Liberties of Stoney Middleton & Eyam, from which mineral duties are due to the Queen in right of her Duchy of Lancaster. The Great Barmote Court for the Low Peak sits annually at Wirksworth Moot Hall, where pride of place goes to a brass standard measuring dish given by Henry VIII.

Totally outside other legal jurisdiction, Barmote Courts elect a Foreman, Steward, 12 jurymen known as the Body of the Mine, and the Barmaster — 'a kind of policeman'. His duties include reporting on the previous year's lead output, settling mining disputes and imposing punishments and fines for mining offences. The Steward presides over the court and must be a barrister of five years' standing or a solicitor of seven years' standing. Although the proceedings of Barmote Courts are now mainly a formality, these are the oldest industrial courts in the world and jealously guard and enforce their unique privileges and laws. The old custom of providing attendees with bread and cheese, clay pipes and tobacco is still observed.

GREAT EASTERN PLANTATION

In 1858, Isambard Kingdom Brunel launched his mighty iron ship The Great Eastern. At 692 ft long with a 118 ft beam,

she was nicknamed the Leviathan and would not be surpassed in size for almost 50 years. Brunel's goal had been to build a ship capable of carrying sufficient coal to enable the vessel to steam to Australia and back without refuelling. Although that venture was dogged by problems, it was The Great Eastern which laid the first successful transatlantic cable, though Brunel did not live to see it. His early death in 1859 was blamed on stress and overwork.

Ashover is about as far from the sea as any village in England but Victorian national pride is reflected here in the Great Eastern Plantation, between the River Amber and the old coach road to Overton. The trees are deciduous: lime, ash, sycamore and elm, laid out to the same dimensions as Brunel's great ship. Though subject to a preservation order, some of the trees have inevitably reached the end of their natural life and a scattering of rotting stumps hide amongst majestic survivors, which from a distance still present a distinctly boat-shaped outline.

GUIDEPOSTS

By an Act of Parliament of 1702, guideposts were to be erected at every crossroads to indicate the next market town reached by each of the four 'joyning highwayes'. The Peak was criss-crossed by networks of

(Bakewell) is built into a wall near Conksbury Bridge, typical of the variety of quaint spellings still legible on many stoops. Others point towards Tidswall, Ashburn, Darby, Worksworth and Chesterfeild Rode. Not all guideposts lie on lonely tracks; some share their sites with modern signposts where ancient crossways have evolved into busy road junctions.

HA-HAs AREN'T FUNNY

This is a funny word for a seriously important feature seen in the grounds of some of our stately homes. A ha-ha is a sunken ditch several feet deep, with a perpendicular stone-faced inner side and a sloping, grassy outer slope. Typically sited between formal gardens and surrounding parkland, a ha-ha was built to keep livestock, especially deer, contained within the park. Unlike a wall, fence or hedge, a ha-ha is hardly noticeable even from a short distance away but blends into the landscape without interrupting the view.

According to La theorie et la pratique du jardinage (Dezallier d'Argenville, 1709) ' ... we frequently make throughviews, call'd Ah, Ah, which are openings in the walls, without grills, to the very level of the walks, with a large and deep ditch at the foot of them, lined on both sides to sustain the earth, and prevent the getting over; which surprises the eye upon coming near it, and makes one cry, Ah! Ah! from whence it takes its name ... it does not at all interrupt the prospect, as the bars of a grill do.'

The design was favoured by leading 18th century landscape gardeners including Lancelot 'Capability' Brown, who created the magnificent Chatsworth park. A ha-ha around the eastern boundary of Edensor is kept in good repair and still stockproof. Chatsworth has at least two more ha-has, while others survive in Derbyshire at Calke Abbey, Kedleston Hall and Sudbury Hall.

HEMLOCK, NOT HORSERADISH

In 1799, an Irish comedian named John Kane, aged 58, was treading the boards and acting as a theatre manager in Buxton.

trading routes which have left us with moorland footpaths branching off in different directions. This is where the more remote stone guideposts have survived, as on Bonsall Moor, Darley Moor, Derwent Moor, Baslow Bar and nearby East Moor, Longstone Edge and several on Beeley Moor.

Some bear dates: 1709 is carved into guideposts including Alport Heights, Pikehall, Curbar Gap and Ball Cross at Bakewell. The Ball Cross post also has direction hands, a not uncommon feature also seen on Beeley Moor and beside the ancient Derby Gate road, west of Bakewell. A guidepost showing Yov (Youlgrave), Bvxt (Buxton), shbvrn (Ashbourne) and Backwel

He had probably taken lodgings in the town and on 10 December prepared himself a meal after gathering what he thought was horseradish. In fact Kane had dug up roots of the deadly hemlock, similar in appearance to those of horseradish, and died in dreadful agony.

Poor John Kane lies buried in the old church of St Anne in Buxton, his gravestone facing west instead of east — supposedly over his feet rather than his head as a final nod to his sense of humour. A beautifully inscribed kerbstone around the grave reads: 'This grave in kind sympathy was restored by John Laurence Toole, one of the eminent comedians of the Victorian era who visited Buxton on August 14th 1889 on the occasion of the opening of the new theatre.'

HERMITAGES

The outcrops of Cratcliffe and Bradley Rocks, with their impressive neighbour, Robin Hood's Stride, stand a short distance from Birchover. An ancient track known as the Portway skirts the area, its history linked to a hermit's cave that lies hidden away at the western base of Cratcliffe Rocks.

Early travellers were dependent upon hospitality along their journey and during the Middle Ages the Church expected this to be provided by hermits. Carved into the rockface inside Cratcliffe cave is a niche — probably for a lamp, and a timeworn 4 ft crucifix in high relief (pictured). Crucifixes were ordered to be provided by, or for, hermits in the 14th century. An external rainwater groove and slots suggest a

former lean-to shelter in front of the cave. The earliest known reference to this hermitage is a Haddon steward's account of 1550 which refers to 'ye harmytt at bradley'.

A lesser-known hermit's cave lies a short distance away at Burycliffe near Gratton, its simple cross carved into the rock behind a natural overhang. Two further rock hermitages lie to the south of the Peak District, at Foremark and Dale Abbey.

HILLFORTS

Our prehistoric forebears found that the landscape of the Peak offered natural strongholds, some of which they enclosed and fortified with at least a single bank and ditch. Finds from the enclosures confirm domestic activity. Hillforts may have been strengthened to protect these settlements from rival tribes, though we have no knowledge as to whether any were besieged. Indeed their main purpose could have been to protect domestic livestock against wild animals.

The largest and highest hillfort in the Peak, at 1,700 ft, is Mam Tor at Castleton, its 16-acre plateau protected by an earthen rampart and ditch some 1,200 yards in circumference. Aerial photographs reveal several hundred 'hut circles' with an average diameter of 23 ft. Aerial photography also confirms evidence of ramparts on the towering promontory of Fin Cop above Monsal Dale. Carl Wark hillfort *(see Carl Wark)* occupies another landmark position with extensive defensive work. Less obvious, smaller hillforts are scattered around the Peak: Castle Naze at Chapel en le Frith, Burr Tor near Camphill at Great Hucklow, Ball Cross at Bakewell, Combes Moss Camp west of Doveholes, and Castle Ring on Harthill Moor — less than an acre in extent yet with two banks and a ditch.

Archaeologists Hart and Makepeace have added a hillfort at Youlgrave to our known sites, naming it Crane's Fort. As with the majority of those named here, it lies on private land. Mam Tor and Carl Wark, however, have public access.

HOB HURST

In days of old, it was as well to keep on the right side of Hob Hurst the giant. Yet as long as a bowl of cream was put out for him, Hob could be of great help on the farm, especially in the dairy. Somehow he would make the butter churn easily and persuade cows to give extra milk. If any corn was found newly threshed in the morning — for Hob worked unseen by night — it exceeded what would have taken ten labourers a whole day to thresh.

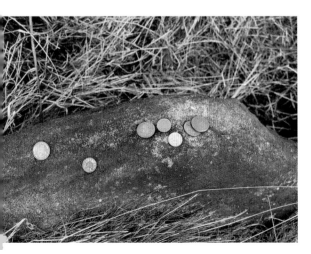

The mythical giant has several Peakland abodes. Hob Hurst's House in Monsal Dale is a massive rocky outcrop with a cave that has given up a skeleton of early date. A Bronze Age burial mound on Harland Edge is also named Hob Hurst's House; excavations of 1853 revealed a layer of charcoal and scorched human bones. Hob has yet another legendary hideaway in Deep Dale near King Sterndale, known as Thirst House Cave. The waters of a nearby spring are supposedly blessed by Hob himself, promising curative powers if taken on Good Friday. As can be seen here, offerings are still left beside at least one of these secretive sites.

HUNTING TOWER

The Chatsworth that we see today replaced an Elizabethan mansion built by Elizabeth Countess of Shrewsbury, 'Bess of Hardwick'. The principal facade of her house was on the opposite side to the present one, approached from the wild East Moor by a steep carriage road that passed close to the hunting tower. From its lofty position on the hillside, the tower enabled noble spectators and their ladies to watch the chase from its latticed windows in comfort. This tall, square building with its rounded corners has survived into the second Elizabethan age and although not open to the public, can be approached from the grounds to give widespread views over Chatsworth and its park to the open countryside beyond.

HYDROPATHY

A new era in health care dawned in England during the 19th century with the introduction of hydropathy. Whereas spas such as Matlock Bath and Buxton had long utilised their thermal springs for internal consumption and bathing, hydropathy was the means of using water to apply external hot or cold treatments.

In the mid-1800s, John Smedley of Lea Mills adapted hydropathy into his innovative Mild Water Cure and founded an establishment on Matlock Bank. Business boomed and others jumped on the bandwagon. The face of Matlock changed

The Liver Pack.

forever as this small market town expanded to accommodate huge numbers of infirm visitors. At least 26 hydros opened up in Matlock alone, with others at Darley Dale, Tansley, Ashover and Baslow. It seems fitting that the last to close, in 1955, was Smedley's Hydropathic Establishment, now County Hall. At one time almost 300 water treatments were on offer in this vast building, although some patients wrote home telling sorry tales of feeling even worse than when they arrived.

ICE HOUSES

If there was any advantage to severe winters pre-electricity, the best people to appreciate it were those with an ice house. It could now be stacked to capacity with thick slabs of pond or river ice. An ice house took the form of a wholly or partly subterranean pit lined with brick or stone, preferably sited in the shade of large trees. Some ice houses were built into earthen banks for maximum insulation, others were

accessible from a small building covered with a mound of earth. A typical, mossy example can be seen just off the road at Hopton Hall.

In a good winter, ice houses were stacked with alternate layers of ice and straw, often packed around joints of meat that would stay frozen right through the following summer. As the months went by, blocks of ice were also taken indoors for keeping pantries cool.

Alton Manor has a large, contemporary 19th century ice house. That of Willersley Castle stands close to a convenient pond. A well preserved example survives in the former grounds of Middleton Hall near Youlgrave; built against a grassy bank, it consists of a short flagged passage that ends at the rim of a stone pit about 20 ft deep. Chatsworth ice house served a useful purpose until the late 1930s, considerably later than most. Probably the largest local ice store was built around 1890 at Darley Dale Hydropathic Establishment, later St Elphin's School and now under redevelopment. It is in effect a ground-level room with thick stone walls and an exceptionally heavy door.

ILLUMINATIONS

Matlock Bath is sometimes dismissed as over-commercialised but its natural scenic beauty is still the greater part of its attraction, and the reason for its popularity in the first place. From late August to the end of October, a touch of magic is brought to this riverside resort through its traditional illuminations, when miles of multicoloured bulbs are reflected in the Derwent. Decorated and illuminated boats glide down the river in the darkness; lights are strung through the trees on the wooded slopes and larger-than-lifesize nursery characters and set pieces line Lovers Walks. Matlock Bath Illuminations have Victorian origins and modern-day preparations utilise some very early glass candle jars.

ILLY WILLY WATER

According to *Lost Beauties of the English Language* (Mackay 1874), illy-willy means malevolent. This definition can hardly be

name to be taken too literally. A storage tank was installed at the head of the brook in the late 1800s to provide pressure for a piped supply. So Illy Willy Water began to flow underground and Chelmorton Docks became as dry as a bone.

INFIDELS' CEMETERY

This neglected little 19th century graveyard lies beside an isolated stretch of the road between Ashford and Monsal Head. Its entrance stones are tumbled and unsafe and sections of a collapsed roadside wall are the only indication that this is anything but a copse. For between the low branches of trees and waist-high weeds can be spotted a few inscribed headstones; others toppled long ago. One epitaph was memorised in his younger days by Frederick James of Bakewell, now in his late eighties:

'Mortal man, wait not for monumental stone
To tell of virtues once by thee possessed
But all around thee make thy goodness known
Ere thou art called to earth's last bed of rest;
And though man's envy may thy worth disown,
Still conscious uprightness shall fill thy breast,
Reward thy life with peace, and make thy memory blest.'

Other epitaphs were recorded by the writer Clarence Daniel, who noted that none of them bore reference to the Bible, God or Jesus Christ — hence the epithet

applied to Illy Willy Water, a brook issuing from the foot of Chelmorton Low. Reliable natural water supplies were at a premium in the White Peak, explaining why Chelmorton village expanded along the line of Illy Willy Water. It used to run down the west side of the main street via open gritstone channels and a series of roadside troughs, serving both domestic and animal needs; the further from the source, the muckier the water. Limestone slabs bridged the brook in front of the cottages. The flow slowed down in summertime, yet people with far poorer supplies came from miles around to fetch water.

Before disappearing into a swallet hole at Town End, the Illy Willy used to deepen and widen out as Chelmorton Docks — not a

Infidels' Cemetery. Yet historical evidence reveals that here lies a small community of local Baptists. Amongst their names are Kitson, White, Skidmore, Shaw, Brushfield, Bramwell and Birley. Sadly, their monuments seem doomed to total dereliction.

INSCRIPTIONS

All sorts of inscriptions occur in unlikely corners of the Peak, generally carved into our hard-wearing gritstone and left as a mark of gratitude. When Edwin Gregory, a mole catcher and devout preacher, recovered from a severe illness in the 1890s, he expressed his gratitude by carving Biblical references, chapter and verse, into several large boulders alongside the road below Curbar Gap.

Lettering on the parapet of Cromford bridge reads: 'The Leap of Mr. B.H. Mare. June 1697'. Descendants of Benjamin Heywood can still recount how he and his favourite mare survived a leap into the Derwent after the horse was startled while crossing the bridge. A similar accident, but which cost the rider his life, is commemorated on the old bridge at Ashford with the simple inscription 'M. Hyde 1664'.

The parish of Middleton and Smerrill has recently revived the tradition of carved inscriptions through its Sites of Meaning Millennium Project, adding inspirational texts to marker stones around the parish boundary. The curved parapet of an old stone bridge in Bradford Dale, for instance, has lines from *The River Duddon* (Wordsworth): 'Still glides the stream, and shall forever glide; the form remains; the function never dies.' The texts all appear together on the Village Stone in Middleton, each orientated towards its parent location on the parish boundary.

JACOBITE REBELLION

Derbyshire was the turning point of the Jacobite Rebellion of 1745, when Prince Charles Edward Stuart marched his army southwards to claim the British throne. On December 4th 'Bonnie Charlie' was proclaimed King in Ashbourne market place

before pressing on to Derby, but within a couple of days was in retreat. Exaggerated tales about his wild and hungry Scots were soon causing panic around the Peak. Farmers at Hope Woodlands buried their valuables; one Eyam family lowered a grandfather clock and other belongings down a lead mine; sheep and cattle were hurriedly driven to isolated folds in the vale of Edale.

The Jacobite cause did have some sympathisers, for the leader of one small party of struggling Highlanders was given treatment and shelter when he broke his leg on Hathersage Moor. Two other stragglers were passed off as sheep drovers and escaped northwards; many years later a claymore and dirk were found near Hathersage.

Shown here is the bronze statue of Bonnie Prince Charlie near Derby Silk Mill.

JACOB'S LADDER

When Jacob Marshall cut a zigzag track from Edale towards Swine's Back in the 18th century, he could not have imagined that walkers would one day climb it for pleasure. Jacob was a travelling salesman who used this important packhorse route across the Dark Peak. Over the course of time, he cut steps into the steep hillside and would send his laden mule by the less arduous but winding track to rejoin him higher up. Nowadays, Jacob's Ladder lies on a stretch of the Pennine Way long distance walk *(qv)*, arguably the most popular route onto the Kinder plateau.

Stoney Middleton also has a Jacob's Ladder — an unpaved track weaving uphill from behind the parish church towards the Eyam road. The climb gives access to other footpaths and offers stunning views over Stoke, Froggatt Edge and Longshaw. This Jacob's Ladder was once part of the daily grind for men and women who walked from outlying hamlets to work in the boot and shoe factories of Stoney Middleton.

JAGGERS

Trains of packhorses and packmules traversed the Peak from the Middle Ages into the 19th century. They were the most common means of transporting goods and were often 40 or 50 animals strong. The man in charge was known as a jagger, from the German 'jaeger', a sturdy breed of horse. A jag was the load which one horse or mule could carry in its twin panniers.

Freight in and out of the Peak included corn, salt, roadstone, malt, wool and cloth, as well as mineral ore carried between mines and smelting mills.

Records from Little Longstone include a document of 1306 referring to a Thomas de jager, and Jagger survives as a well-known surname today. Two fields near Harborough Rocks are named Jaggerways and elsewhere in the Peak are a Jaggers Gate, Jaggers Clough and several Jagger Lanes. This road sign stands above Brockhurst near Ashover.

JAILS & LOCK-UPS

Derbyshire had its first official jail around 1550. In earlier times, miscreants were imprisoned by their 'betters' in such strongholds as Peveril Castle at Castleton *(qv)*. The Poor Law of 1601 introduced Houses of Correction, supervised by a master who meted out punishments as he saw fit. One such establishment, in reality a single cell barely six feet square, was set up at Tideswell in 1711, twice moving into

larger premises. By the mid-17th century, Wirksworth had a House of Correction but it fell into disuse until desperate neighbouring towns and villages demanded its reinstatement in 1727.

Lock-ups were very small, temporary prisons for holding offenders en route for the magistrates, though more often used as an overnight cooler for drunks. Many parish prisons were abandoned when the new County Jail opened at Derby in 1827. Original lock-ups survive at Ticknall, Smisby and Alfreton and, seen here, the rather larger Cromford lock-up prior to renovation by the Arkwright Society.

JERUSALEM BUILDED HERE

At Ladmanlow, near Burbage stands a row of stone houses known locally as Jerusalem Terrace, its name attributed to a Biblical connection. An early resident of one of these cottages was a popular and much-loved preacher, who so frequently referred to Jerusalem in his sermons and texts that local folk called the whole terrace by this name. Similarly, the meadow opposite became Jerusalem meadow. Whatever their original place-names, they are now long forgotten.

K6

Villages which have managed to keep their traditional red telephone kiosks are generally in country areas where modernisation might jar on the eye. A rather special version in Bonsall Dale is the classic K6 or Jubilee model, designed by architect Sir Giles Gilbert Scott to commemorate the Silver Jubilee of King George V in 1935. Its official description is 'a square cast iron kiosk with domed roof. Unperforated crowns to top panels and margin glazing to windows and doors'. This design was updated from the red painted K2, for which Scott had won a competition organised by the Royal Fine Art Commission in 1924. K6 was 25% lighter than the K2 but still weighed around three-quarters of a ton. Within five years of its introduction, 20,000 K6 kiosks had been erected across the length and breadth of Britain, with thousands more to follow.

KINDER SCOUT

The highest point in Derbyshire lies 2,088 ft (636 m) above sea-level on the sombre Kinder Scout plateau. The word Kinder has Celtic origins, while Scout comes from the Old Norse 'skuti' — a projecting cliff. Ask people what they know about Kinder Scout and some will tell you that it shares its latitude with Siberia; avid walkers know it as the start/finish of the Pennine Way (qv); historians might speak of the many aircraft wrecks littering Kinder and Bleaklow.

What is not so widely known is that this magnificent wilderness is considered to be a Holy Mountain, regularly visited by pilgrims from The Aetherius Society, a spiritual organisation with members worldwide. In a mission known as Operation Starlight, 19 mountains around the world have been charged with 'very high frequency spiritual energies'. Kinder Scout is one of the sites chosen for this special role; the charging took place at the highest point on 31 January 1959. The UK also has Holy Mountains in Scotland, Wales,

Dartmoor and Devon. Others around the world include Mont Blanc and Kilimanjaro, with two in Australia, one in New Zealand and four in America.

KING STONE

Stanton Moor near Birchover is rich in prehistoric sites, with over 70 Bronze Age cairns and five embanked or stone circles. The best known of the stone circles, the Nine Ladies, has a single outlier 130 ft to the south-west, approximately three feet high and known as the King Stone. Nine Ladies lines up via the King Stone with a natural rock called the Andle Stone and onwards to Doll Tor stone circle, on the western side of Stanton Moor. The mysterious King Stone also marks the mid-point between two embanked circles.

As Christianity reached the Peak, legends came into being that scared away remnants of the old pagan beliefs. Tellers of tales used to relate that the nine boulders on Stanton Moor had once been maidens, turned to stone for eternity as punishment for dancing on the Sabbath *(see Nine Naughty Ladies and a Fiddler)*. The solitary King Stone had been their fiddler or, say some, a pagan priest.

KING STREET

Any thoroughfare named King Street suggests either a royal connection or considerable importance as a well travelled route; Roman 'streets' can be hundreds of miles long. The latter ancestry can hardly account for King Street in Youlgrave, more a steep alleyway than a road at all, and not even named on the Ordnance Survey Street Atlas. A little delving on the local scene reveals that generations of villagers have understood the king in question to be Charles II, though no one seems to know why.

KIOSKS

Chelmorton has the rare privilege of a unique telephone kiosk, not a modern glass booth nor even the familiar red box that has received special dispensation in other Peak villages *(see K6)*. Chelmorton telephone kiosk was constructed in 1933 to blend in with its White Peak surroundings. Built to standard size from concrete blocks beneath a slated roof, it cost £18. The limestone-coloured kiosk stands beside the main road through the village and is unlikely to be uprooted for any newfangled, mass produced replacement.

KNIGHTS OF OLD

Effigies of bold knights lie in many Peakland churches. Some of their number fell in battle, one or two died in considerable disgrace, but most reached a peaceful old age. Just a few that are worthy of mention include a 12th century crusader in All Saints Church, Youlgrave and a recumbent stone effigy in St Helen's Church, Darley Dale, depicting Sir John de Darley who died in 1322. Alabaster has also provided some particularly fine carvings, notably a late 14th century monument in Bakewell All Saints' Church commemorating Sir Godfrey Foljambe and his wife, Lady Avena. Here too are other knights in armour, including Sir George Vernon of Haddon Hall and Sir Thomas de Wendesley, who died fighting for his king in 1403. Again at Youlgrave is the exquisite miniature effigy of Thomas Cokayne, killed in a quarrel in 1488 *(pictured)*, also a later wall monument depicting Roger Rowe in armour and ruffs.

Wirksworth parish church contains the fine altar tomb of Anthony Lowe, a 16th century knight who was servant to four consecutive English sovereigns. The brave knights of Hathersage can actually be seen in shining armour, depicted alongside their fashionable ladies on the famed memorial brasses inside St Michael & All Saints' parish church.

LEASH FEN

Between Big Moor and East Moor, north-east of Baslow, lie a few square miles of marshy cotton-grass moorland, the subject of a strange folk-rhyme:

'When Chesterfield was heath and broom
Leash Fen was a market town,
Now Leash Fen is sunken down
And Chesterfield a market town.'

Nothing more than a few tantalising clues
support the tradition of a town buried
beneath the swampy waste, intersected by
lethargic brooks and encircled by ancient
boundary crosses. Yet when a drainage
trench was cut across Leash Fen in the
1830s, workers found fragments of crude
earthenware and many pieces of black oak
preserved in the peat, described as
'squared and cut by some instrument.'
Signs of early cultivation had been noted
some 20 years earlier.

Whether or not the site of a lost market
town, Leash Fen has not always been
'sunken down' and of little worth, for
environmental core samples taken in recent
years have provided archaeologists with
evidence of mixed arable and pastoral
farming separated by areas of woodland,
beginning in the second and continuing
through the first millennium BC.

LEPERS' LEGACIES

During the Middle Ages, the dreaded
disease of leprosy was known in England.
Sufferers were obliged to warn of their
approach by ringing a clapper or bell and
had to hide their offensive deformities
under a hooded cloak and a pair of oxhide
boots. The only compassionate care for
lepers was provided by monks. Between
the 12th and 15th centuries, monastic
houses established over 200 leper hospitals
in England. Those closest to the Peak were
at Chesterfield, in the area still known as
Spital, and Derby.

'Leprosie' was just one of the diseases
reportedly cured at St Anne's Well in Buxton
during Tudor times. A further Derbyshire
reference appears in Bakewell Vestry
Accounts of 1698: 'Pd for a warrant for ye
Lepers 1/-'. (One shilling, now 5p.)

The Eyre Arms at Hassop claims a 'lepers'
sill' in a former external rear wall.
Generations of landlords have inherited the
belief that this is where disfigured
customers were served with their ale, well
out of sight of healthier tipplers. Similarly, a

narrow window in the east wall of
St Helen's Church at Darley Dale is often
described as a lepers' window, where
afflicted worshippers could participate in
services at a safe distance.

Tradition has it that a crusader who
returned to his native Stoney Middleton
with leprosy was cured by bathing in a
thermal spring. He erected a nearby chapel
in thanksgiving, dedicated to St Martin,
patron saint of both soldiers and cripples.
St Martin's church later replaced the chapel.

LEY LINES

Whatever the true significance of
prehistoric sites and monuments around
the Peak, a good number seem to be
interconnected by invisible straight lines
which are part of a countrywide network,
believed by some to share a mysterious
power source. These so-called 'ley lines'
have been researched since the early

20th century and are found to connect or intersect at stone circles, cairns, tumuli, standing stones, crosses and also Christian churches — often built on sites once sacred to pagan religion.

The churches of Matlock, Bonsall, Brassington, Bradbourne and Fenny Bentley lie on a distinctive church alignment. Up to 150 ley lines are claimed to intersect Arbor Low, linking this important stone circle with churches including Parwich, Monyash, Ashford in the Water and Elton, along with Nine Ladies circle on Stanton Moor, Pilsbury Castle near Hartington, and scores of tumuli. Further intriguing patterns can be revealed by taking a ruler and pencil to a large-scale map of the White Peak.

LITTLE JOHN'S GRAVE

A writer of 60 years ago describes annual pilgrimages to Hathersage church by members of the Ancient Order of Foresters Friendly Society. Dressed in Lincoln green and red, participants laid a wreath on a grave that they had taken into their care, marked: 'Here lies buried Little John, The Friend and Lieutenant of Robin Hood'.

The story goes that Little John was a native of Hathersage, who returned to die at his birthplace — a cottage which stood near Hathersage church into the 1800s. One of its last occupants used to tell how in her younger days, Little John's grave was opened up to reveal the remains of a man eight feet tall. She and other villagers could also recall the disappearance from the church of the outlaw's green cap and yew longbow. Both items were moved some

time prior to restoration work in 1851. During this restoration, the upper half of a stone slab was discovered beneath the church floor. It had been put to use for two interments; the later, post-14th century inscription reads simply 'L.J.'

LOVERS' LEAPS

Many a tale of unrequited love ends with a desperate final leap from some great height and the Peak has at least four Lovers' Leaps. Lovers' Leap rock in Dovedale carries the tale of a jilted maid who threw herself from this lofty tor, only to land in thick bushes that broke her fall. Equally lucky was Hannah Baddaley, who in 1762, spurned and heartbroken, climbed an 80 ft cliff in Stoney Middleton gorge and jumped straight into local legend. Miraculously saved by her billowing petticoats and a cluster of brambles, Hannah apparently suffered only cuts and bruises. Nevertheless, she was still only 26 when her burial was recorded in the parish register two years later.

E.L.S.17944. Lovers Leap, Stoney Middleton

The tradition behind Lovers' Leap in Ashwood Dale tells of a daring feat of horsemanship which took an eloping couple beyond the reach of a posse of angry relatives. The lovers were desperately racing to reach the famous 'runaway weddings' church at Peak Forest, where they could be married at any time of day or night, without banns. Galloping towards Ashwood Dale, one of their horses cast a shoe, forcing the couple to share the other horse. In spite of its double burden their

LITTLE JOHNS GRAVE, HATHERSAGE CHURCHYARD PEAK DISTRICT - PR JAY

mount was urged to leap the gorge. Horse and riders landed safely but not a single pursuer was brave enough to follow suit.

A very silly lovelorn wench gave her name to Jane Hambleton's Rock in Lathkill Dale. Jane was bidden by her lover to prove her love — and win his hand in marriage — by throwing herself from this vertical crag. Not only did she comply, even landing safely, but repeated the exploit on demand. Still with nothing worse to show than a broken finger, she was commanded by her beau to jump for a third time. Sure enough, Jane Hambleton was soon making a trip down the aisle — but in a shroud, not a bridal gown.

LUTUDARUM

Tangible evidence of Roman lead mining in the Peak comes from a number of lead ingots, called pigs, which have come to light during the past two centuries or so. The first to be identified was found on Cromford Moor in 1777. Inscribed IMP CAES HADRIANA AUG MET LUT it can be dated with accuracy to the reign of the Roman Emperor Hadrian, AD117-138. The letters LUT, however, set a puzzle that remains unsolved — the lost location of Lutudarum.

Wirksworth, Matlock and Chesterfield are favoured contenders for the site but since the letters LUT, LUTUD or LUTUDARES distinguish pigs of lead found all over Derbyshire — along with others found further afield and obviously lost en route for the ports — Lutudarum may have been the entire lead-producing field centred on the Peak. Pigs of lead and a wealth of other related finds can be seen in both Buxton Museum and the Peak District Mining Museum at Matlock Bath.

MAIDENS' GARLANDS

The Peak still has a few examples of an ancient floral tradition which died out almost two centuries ago. The parish churches of Ashford, Matlock and Ilam all display time-darkened crantsies, or maidens' garlands, symbols of purity carried at the funerals of young unmarried women. Made by friends and family of the deceased, these melancholy tributes

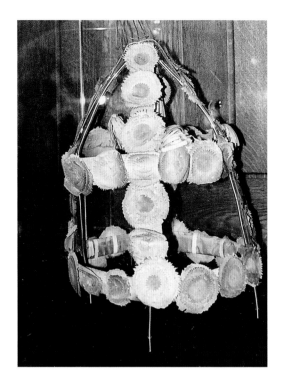

usually consist of a hooped wickerwork frame decorated with ribbons, rosettes and flowers, all made from folded or crimped white paper. A paperwork centrepiece such as a collar, pair of gloves or handkerchief was sometimes inscribed with a text chosen by the dying girl herself. After the burial service the garland was hung over her pew, although the last to be made at Eyam, in 1840, was buried with the coffin.

For all their apparent fragility, maidens' garlands would have survived in far greater numbers but for being thrown out when 'new brooms' swept through old churches. In 1749, the churchwardens of Hope paid one shilling and sixpence 'for removing ye Garlands to make ye Church lighter.'

The largest surviving collection of garlands in the Peak is preserved at St Giles' Church, Matlock. Six in number, they are now kept out of direct light, with the exception of one recently conserved relic inside a perspex case *(pictured)*.

Exceptionally, a maiden's garland was created in recent years as a special tribute at the funeral at Ashford of Miss Joy Price, Franciscan Tertiary and former Sunday School teacher at Ashford Holy Trinity church.

MARBLE BRIDGES

One aspiring village in the Peak has boasted its own royal family, albeit only on account of their surname. Certainly the Princes used to be at the top of the social scale in Bonsall and their name provided a useful 'put down' when a local man, far from home, was mocked for his country ways. He was treated with new respect when he described his home town as the seat of worthy Princes, with 'two hundred marble arches' in front of the residents' homes. True enough, for until Miss A.R. Prince paid for Bonsall brook to be culverted in 1871, its waters ran alongside the main street, spanned by slabs of smooth, white limestone in front of the cottages. Shown here is a 'marble bridge' where Bonsall brook still flows above ground, higher up the village.

MARKET HALLS

The right to hold a weekly market was granted to many Peakland villages from the 13th century onwards. Although only a handful of regular markets survive, evidence of others can be seen in their ancient market crosses and market halls. Bakewell still has both a thriving market and a picturesque gabled market hall, now a Tourist Information Centre.

In 1906, the centuries-old market hall at Winster became the first National Trust property in Derbyshire. The building had recently been restored, with the open arches which once sheltered traders and their wares filled in for strength. Eyam has a tiny stone market hall behind the village stocks, both features long obsolete by the time busy Longnor opened a new market hall in 1873. This building still displays a list of charges, such as one penny for every pig sold at Longnor market.

MEMORIAL BRASSES

Whilst some memorial brasses are unburnished and tarnished with age, others gleam from centuries of polishing. Simple images can occasionally be made out on modest brass tablets, as at Baslow, Beeley and Hartington, whereas other miniature brasses were obviously professionally engraved, for example the quaintly-costumed figures of Latham Woodroffe in Bakewell church *(pictured)* and Henry Balguy at Hope. Youlgrave parish church contains a lovely, rare brass to a spinster.

By contrast, a lady who shares a memorial brass with her husband at Taddington wears a mourning mantle, denoting a vow of widowhood. Tideswell parish church has many notable brasses, including a Knight Constable and a robed and bejewelled Bishop. Equally fine costume detail is seen on the famous Eyre brasses in Hathersage church, engraved with images of medieval knights and their ladies.

MERMAIDS

Mermaids have a firm place in folklore even this far inland — all they need is a watery abode in some isolated, lonely spot. Mermaid's Pool on Kinder Scout is home to a capricious occupant who may surface and drag you down if you try to gaze into the depths of her domain. Yet if she is visited at midnight on Easter Eve, and if the mood takes her, she might invest you with the gift of long life.

Legends have surrounded a 'bottomless pool' near the Mermaid Inn on the moors between Buxton and Leek for hundreds of years. Local belief holds that no bird or animal will drink here. There is also a conviction that the pool never freezes over, however severe the winter, nor does the level fall when all around is parched. One very old story tells how a certain Joshua Linnet kidnapped a beautiful woman who spurned his persistent advances. She was tied up and thrown into the Mermaid Pool, screaming out as she drowned that she would be avenged and would haunt the place forever. Three days later, the body of Joshua Linnet was found in the pool, his face gashed by long, deep scratches. Before long the promised haunting started with a vengeance, from tales of people disappearing without trace to violent attacks and murders. One victim had a narrow escape after a tippler in the Cock Inn accepted a five shilling dare to visit the haunted pool in the dark. As he drew nearer, he heard the cries of a female in distress and discovered a man trying to drown a young woman. It transpired that she had been seduced by her attacker and was not intended to live to tell the tale.

A successful murder is firmly set in 1679, when a woman pedlar was strangled and robbed on her way from Leek to Bakewell market. Her body was thrown into Mermaid Pool. A man named Andrew Simpson was arrested for the crime and confessed to two other robberies with violence.

The diminutive mermaid seen here is preserved at Buxton Museum, though where and when she was captured nobody knows. There is still skin on her yellowing bones and scales on her tail. One arm is raised in the traditional pose of combing her tresses, sadly no longer luxuriant after many years out of water. A rictal grin hints at some deception from her fishy past.

MILESTONES

Buxton Museum also displays the oldest milestone in the Peak, a Roman relic showing 11 miles to the fort at Navio, present-day Brough. A Roman mile of 1,000 paces was slightly shorter than the later

Also now bereft of traffic is a rusting iron milepost beside the old Mam Tor road at Castleton, a route that finally had to be closed after an interminable battle with subsidence.

MILK & HONEY LINE

Ongoing work promises to restore Ecclesbourne Valley Railway, the Duffield/Wirksworth branch line through the lovely route of the River Ecclesbourne. Opened in 1867, this became known as the Milk and Honey line, transporting milk and produce from local farms and breathing life into the agricultural community. With direct freight lines into local quarries, the railway also transported enormous quantities of stone until the track became dormant in 1989.

The line carried passengers for 80 years and Ecclesbourne Valley Railway Association has already restored passenger travel to the first few miles of the Milk and Honey line. Trains begin their scenic journey at Wirksworth station, chugging southwards as the route is gradually returned to full service, destination Duffield via Idridgehay, Shottle and Hazelwood. Reminiscences and yarns from ex-railway workers recall milk trains, weedkiller trains and runaway trains. Dripping rail tunnels still burrow below Wirksworth itself, a small town with a huge debt to its Milk and Honey Line.

MIND YOUR MANNERS

Many a tale revolves around our old inns, from riots and revolutions to murders, but a story on a lighter note concerns a hanging sign outside The Manners in Bakewell. This inn takes its name from the family which owns nearby Haddon Hall. Unfortunately, at its last renovation but one, The Manners sign was mistakenly painted to show the Cavendish arms, borne by the Dukes of Devonshire of nearby Chatsworth. The error went unnoticed until a member of the Manners family called in to point it out. The brewery was in no hurry to right the mistake and it was several years later before a brand new sign went up, in 2006, showing the Manners peacock instead of the Cavendish serpent.

English mile, this dictated by the length of a barleycorn at three to the inch.

Later guideposts often showed directions without distances but true milestones became essential as roads improved. They invariably give the distance to London as well as to the closest towns, as seen on an uninterrupted series placed a mile apart along the A6 through Darley Dale. Some are stone, others are the later, cast-iron type. A milestone dated 1801 was left in place to become part of the wall around the thermal fishpond in Matlock Bath. Long years of lying below water-level have taken their toll; the wording is now so faint as to be illegible. We can still read the original inscription as emphasised on a photograph taken many years ago by Frank Rodgers for *More Curiosities of Derbyshire & The Peak District.*

MURDER STONES

On a roadside embankment at Nab End, Rainow, stands a neatly inscribed stone with a mysterious tale to tell: 'Here John Turner was cast away in a heavy snow storm in the night in or about the year 1755'. The night was in fact Christmas Eve, though the correct year is believed to be 1735. But no-one was ever able to explain the enigmatic postscript on the other side of the stone: 'The print of a woman's shoe was found by his side in the snow were [sic] he lay dead'.

Another lonely death involving certain foul play is commemorated on the Murder Stone near Disley. It is inscribed: 'WILLIAM WOOD Eyam Derbyshire Here MURDERED July 16th A.D. 1823 Prepare to meet Thy God'. Wood was a 32-year-old weaver of Eyam with a wife and three children. On the day of his death he was returning on foot from Manchester after selling some of his cloth and was carrying the large sum of

£70. Along the way, he bought drinks at an inn for three men who then followed him, stole his money and beat him to death with a large rock.

Some months later, a man named Charles Taylor was arrested when he tried to pass one of the stolen notes in Macclesfield. He confessed to the murder and named his two accomplices as Dale and Platt. The former was brought to justice and executed on 21 April 1824 at Chester City Gaol. Taylor died from self-inflicted injuries following a failed suicide attempt. Platt was never caught.

A legend about the murder spot tells how William Wood's skull imprinted a large hollow into the ground where he fell. Thereafter, it always opened up again if attempts were made to fill it in, nor would anything grow there. Many years after the murder, a local man repeatedly tried to pack the hole with stones but they always went missing.

NEEDLES & PINS

Peakland gritstone has sustained a great variety of industries both at home and overseas. A particularly fine type of gritstone produced grindstones for specific trades at Hathersage into the early years of the past century. The main local employment here was wire drawing, alongside the allied manufacture of needles and pins, hackles and gills, metal buttons and cast-steel wire, but all at a price — Hathersage was renowned for its permanently dusty, unhealthy air.

As early as 1810, a needle maker named Samuel Cocker was in business at Hathersage, to be followed by many others. Robert Cook and Company, one of only three firms worldwide to produce hackle pins for combing wool, was the last to close down during the early 1900s. By this time, stringent working regulations were coming into force to combat the lethal effects of inhaling dust and metal filings, so Hathersage gradually came clean. Some of the old factory buildings now serve commercial and residential use, with a couple of the mill chimneys left standing.

NELSON'S COLUMN

Sixty-two years after Admiral Lord Nelson fell at the Battle of Trafalgar, along with more than 1,580 fellow British sailors, the famous Nelson's Column was erected in London. Yet in 1810, only five years after Trafalgar, a memorial obelisk to Nelson was erected on Birchen Edge near Baslow. Its gritstone shaft is topped by a stone finial ball and each side of the obelisk faces a cardinal point of the compass. The eastern side is inscribed 'A.D. Nelson. Died Oct 21, 1805' with the later addition of the centenary year. The stonemason, John Brightman, left his initials on the opposite side. About 100 feet away stand three large natural rocks, shaped by nature to resemble ships' prows and carved with the names of three British fighting vessels: Victory, Defiance and Royal Soverin [sic].

NEOLITHIC MONUMENTS

By around 3500-3000 BC, our Neolithic ancestors were widely settled on the limestone uplands of the Peak. Evidence of their occupation ranges from the great henges of Arbor Low and the Bull Ring to tiny artefacts and tools. These early farmers made the move from food gathering to food production and their scattered settlements have revealed polished stone axe heads, a hammer head of local basalt, flint knives and scrapers, pottery sherds and flint arrowheads. Their tumuli and chambered tombs are to be found on high ground in the southern White Peak including Bole Hill, Ringham Low, Green Low, Stoney Low, Harborough Rocks, Minninglow and Five Wells (pictured). The word 'low' derives from 'hlaew', the Anglo-Saxon word for a mound.

Chambered tombs were used for several interments. Five Wells revealed 12 skeletons when excavated in 1846 by Bateman, with a further five awaiting discovery. The dead were placed in stone slab chambers connected by similarly constructed passages, the entire structure capped by massive limestone slabs overlaid with an oval mound of earth. Natural caves and rock shelters were also used for interments; a cave near Longnor gave up four Neolithic human skeletons and one of a dog. The humans at least had been laid to rest in ritual fashion.

NINE NAUGHTY LADIES & A FIDDLER

Unlike the limestone henge monument of Arbor Low (qv), many smaller stone circles

of the Peak are built from gritstone. One of the best preserved is the Nine Ladies on Stanton Moor, with its outlying King Stone to the south-west and standing north of around 70 Bronze Age cairns. Thirty-three feet in diameter, the circle of nine upright stones is set in a low bank that originally enclosed a central cairn. Legend has it that these boulders were once nine maidens, turned to stone for naughtily dancing on the Sabbath *(also see King Stone)*.

Nineteenth-century archaeologists opened up cairns on Stanton Moor to discover human remains accompanied by distinctive clay urns, giving rise to the popular term Beaker People. Their decorated vessels represent a considerable advance in pottery making, while the existence of grave goods indicates a belief in the afterlife. Some beakers contained traces of food or drink; others were cinerary urns.

NOTICEBOARDS

Village noticeboards are nothing new, though nowadays they tend to display

coming events rather than the type of admonishments found on some old signs which still lay down the law. A notice fixed to a tree in Lathkill Dale advises walkers that they are following a concessionary footpath which may oblige them to pay for the privilege. It reads 'No public road. This footpath is open to visitors except Thursdays in Easter Week. Toll on that day 1 penny each person'.

Strangers entering Alport near Youlgrave should take heed of a strict warning attached to a roadside building. Headed 'Vagrancy Act 1824' the board is kept in good repair (just in case) and pronounces that 'All Vagabonds found lodging or begging within this hamlet will be taken up and dealt with as the LAW directs'.

Tansley, it seems, has different concerns. A Victorian notice-board on the outer wall of a house on Church Street spells out a stern anti-litter warning by order of Albert Toft, Inspector of Nuisances for the Bakewell Union Rural Sanitary Authority. Dated 'Feby 20th 1885' it informs that 'NOTICE is hereby given that any Person or Persons found depositing any Refuse, or other matter injurious to health in any Public thoroughfare will be prosecuted as the law directs'. And at the time of writing, there is not a single scrap of litter in sight.

OCTAGONAL CHURCH & CHIPPY

The church of St Martin at Stoney Middleton retains the tower of an earlier edifice, said to have been built by Joan Eyre in thanksgiving for the safe return of her husband from the 1415 Battle of Agincourt. When the main body of the church was rebuilt in 1759, it was given an unusual octagonal nave. Church historian Dr Charles Cox subsequently grumbled that the architect — who also designed the majestic stables at Chatsworth and Buxton — would have been better 'to confine his talents exclusively to secular work'. The octagonal theme in St Martin's is echoed in the shape of its stone font and the pattern of central floor tiles.

It can be only a coincidence that the old Stoney Middleton toll house, now a busy fish and chip shop, is also octagonal. Built of gritstone with a slate roof, this quaint building was constructed in 1840 at a cost of £87.15s, for occupation as a toll house on the Chesterfield/Hernstone Lane Head turnpike. It was obviously expedient for the keeper to have walls, and hence windows, facing in different directions.

ODIN MINE

Tradition has it that this Castleton lead mine was worked as a penal settlement under the invading Norsemen, who named it after their mythological giver of victory. The earliest reference to the place seems to date from 1280, when a man was put on trial for poaching hereabouts, well within the bounds of the Royal Forest of the Peak (*qv*). The first record of mining activity at Odin dates to almost four centuries later. Lead production increased steadily, to peak between the 1720s and around 1800. Some 100 men, women and children worked as much as 800 tons of lead ore a year. Each ton also produced around three ounces of silver. The mineral resin elaterite, commonly termed elastic bitumen, was first discovered here.

The lead mine closed in the mid-19th century but sections remain accessible to experienced cavers via the man-made Odin Gorge. A gritstone crushing wheel and its 18 ft diameter iron track are preserved beside the old Mam Tor road, almost opposite the former entrance to the main haulage level.

OIL WELLS

The Peak District is not an obvious place to be associated with oil production, yet in the 1930s drilling took place at Rushton, where the D'Arcy Exploration Company erected a 136 ft derrick on Gun Hill. Recalling his experiences in Around Rushton, former employee Peter Jones describes working on the derrick in 1938: 'The operation ran day and night on a three shift system ... working up there, 80 ft up in the air, on top of Gun Hill in winter wasn't a job many fancied.' Eventually, however, when drilling reached 4,500 ft and encountered a flow of fresh water, it became clear that there was

no point in continuing and Gun Hill oil well was abandoned.

The country's first inland oil well was sunk at Hardstoft, near Tibshelf in Derbyshire. Explorations for oil started in England during WW1, with the North Derbyshire Coalfield identified as a possible mainland source. On 27 May 1919, oil was struck at Hardstoft at a depth of 3,070 ft. More than 2,500 tons were produced over the next nine years. Meanwhile, ownership rights had come under dispute and Hardstoft Oil Well was in effect taken over in March 1923 by the Duke of Devonshire, owner of the mineral rights and the land on which the well had been sunk.

In 1934, the Petroleum Production Act vested British oil ownership in the Crown, with the exception of three existing licensees, one of whom was the Duke of Devonshire in respect of Hardstoft. His oil well ceased production in 1945 and was finally capped in 1952. The site is now occupied by the Oilwells Nursery. Its old wellhead still seeps a puddle of 'Tibshelf Crude' and visitors with a keen nose will pick up a distinctive smell wafting on the breeze.

OKER HILL

A Victorian guide book to The Matlocks claims that Oker derives its name from the Latin 'occursus', meaning conflict. Other early writers suggested that the occupying

ORE HOUSE

Ore means mainly one thing in the Peak and that is lead ore — galena. Newly extracted ore underwent a number of processes, including the all-essential weighing, but in the meantime had to be kept secure, especially at the end of a working day. This was the purpose of the Ore House at Winster, a squat, flat-roofed stone building which served as a type of night-safe. Just visible within is a chute, through which ore was tipped from the outside to be kept temporarily under lock and key.

Romans had built a fort on Oker Hill from which to 'intimidate the Britons'. But proof is elusive and this solitary peak between Matlock and Darley is better famed as the inspiration for *The Keepsake*, composed by Wordsworth in 1838. The sonnet relates a legend about two brothers, who each planted a sycamore on the summit of the hill before parting for ever. One brother made a success of his life and his tree thrived; the other met only with failure and his tree followed suit:
'The trees grew,
And now entwine their arms,
But ne'er again embraced those brothers.'
   Another story claims that it was a local man named Shore who planted the twin trees to provide, in due course of time, the wood for his coffin. Nevertheless, one of the two original sycamores still stands untouched. Its companion did not reach maturity, nor did a successor planted in 1902, but the most recently planted sapling has become well established within sight of its unmistakable 'big brother' landmark.

OWL HOLES

Renovation of our traditional stone barns occasionally ensures the survival of an owl hole. These apertures allow easy access and nesting opportunities to birds known for their efficient pest control, to the benefit of both farmers and owls, if not so good for rodents. The owl hole seen here is the smaller opening, spotted on an old stone barn near Darley Bridge.
   The caving fraternity knows Owl Hole as a 50 ft deep open pothole (with a lower

passage named Owl's Bottom) in the upper Dove area above Dowel Dale. In recent years, Owl Hole has undergone a great deal of clearance, including tons of dumped rubbish, enabling new passages to be opened up and explored. From a cave once considered 'lost' to cavers, the Owl Hole system now has over 200 yards of surveyed passage with many chambers and fine formations. The full story can be read online at www.deeppenetration.info

PACKHORSE BRIDGES

A number of picturesque packhorse bridges are still crossed by foot in the Peak, though now for pleasure. Built from the Middle Ages onwards, they lay on busy trading routes, along which such necessities as salt, wool, malt, leather, lead and cloth were transported by trains of packhorses. Each animal was laden with a balanced pair of panniers, so bridge parapets needed to be very low. Some packhorse bridges were also exceedingly narrow *(see Viator's Bridge)*. One of only 27 inches spans the River Noe at Edale, similar in width to the 17th century Holme Bridge on the Wye in Bakewell.

Derbyshire and Staffordshire are linked by packhorse bridges on the Dove, whilst Cheshire, Derbyshire and Staffordshire come together near the lonely Pannier's Pool packhorse bridge at Three Shires Head *(qv)*. The pretty hump-backed bridge seen here is tucked away in peaceful retirement in Bradford Dale, whereas the impounding of 20th century reservoirs led to the resiting of both Goyt packhorse bridge and that of

Derwent Woodlands. The medieval stonework of the latter was reconstructed at Slippery Stones.

PADLEY CHAPEL

Padley Hall, near Grindleford, was held into the 16th century by the Fitzherberts, staunch Catholics — a dangerous faith to practise in early Elizabethan England. The Hall was regularly raided for evidence of Catholic worship until, in July 1588, two priests were discovered hiding within its walls and taken prisoner. Nicholas Garlick and Robert Ludlam were found guilty of high treason and, along with Richard Sympson who shared their faith, were hanged, drawn and quartered at Derby

PADLEY CHAPEL Nr GRINDLEFORD C41

before the month was out; their butchered remains were stuck onto poles on St Mary's Bridge.

Although Padley Hall fell into ruin, its domestic chapel, originally the upper floor of the gatehouse, remained standing and served for many years as a farm building. In 1933 it was restored as a Roman Catholic chapel, the altar having been retrieved from the nearby ruins. The three martyred priests are commemorated in an annual July pilgrimage and celebration of Holy Mass at Padley Chapel.

PENNINE WAY

The southern end of the Pennine Way, Britain's first long-distance footpath, lies at Edale, from where walkers heading northwards are almost immediately faced with the formidable Kinder plateau before threading onwards along the Pennine ridge — 'the backbone of England'. After 268 miles, the journey ends at Kirk Yetholm over the Scottish border. En route it passes through three national parks and countless places of interest including Hebden Bridge, Haworth, the Settle/Carlisle Railway and the Roman site of Housesteads. The ultimate challenge is to complete the entire route with night-stops but many walkers take it a stretch at a time.

The thousands who tread the Pennine Way every year owe thanks to Tom Stephenson, former secretary of the Ramblers' Association, whose vision of a continuous footpath took 30 years of negotiation, to be finally realised on 24 April 1965.

PETRIFYING WELLS

Almost forgotten now, even in Matlock Bath where they used to attract thousands of trippers a year — including the future Queen Victoria — these damp and fascinating grottoes are now represented by one lone active survivor at Matlock Bath Aquarium. Also known as dripping wells, petrifying wells utilised the same process that formed the natural beds of tufa in the vicinity of Matlock Bath. Any object placed under a constant spray of the local, heavily mineralised water becomes gradually

coated with calcium carbonate, building up in thickness until it is apparently turned to stone (see Tufa Stone).

Local shops sold petrified objects as souvenirs. Particular favourites were ferns, kettles, shoes, hats, toys and birds' nests complete with eggs — the one shown here is displayed in Buxton Museum. Shopkeepers in Matlock Bath still answer a steady stream of enquiries about the old petrifying wells, sought in vain by visitors who remember their damp magic from their childhood. A disused tufa-built petrifying well is one of the features in Derwent Gardens.

PEVERIL CASTLE

Otherwise known as Peak Castle, this Castleton landmark was built around 1070/80 by William Peveril, bastard son of William the Conqueror. The keep was added in 1176. Almost a hundred years later, one John de Nedham was imprisoned within its walls, whereas his companion, Hubert the Robber, was hanged. In 1403, a man from Little Longstone was incarcerated here and starved for six days; his right hand was cut off before he was set free.

Peveril Castle gradually reached the end of its useful life and three centuries later was in ruins. Visitors can explore the keep with its rare garderobe (qv) — one of the oldest lavatories in the country.

PILSBURY CASTLE

This motte and bailey castle, north-west of Hartington, is accessible on foot. Constructed on a knoll, its boundaries are protected by man-made banks and external ditches, with a natural limestone reef to the east. Evidence for a probable earth and timber castle survives as a circular mound — the motte, and twin enclosures — the baileys. The fortification cannot be accurately dated and may have its origins in unsettled Saxon times, perhaps even earlier. Pilesberie, as recorded in the Domesday Survey, is a name of Saxon derivation.

A detailed survey coupled with intensive documentary research has been carried out by Arteamus (Archaeological Research Team, University of Sheffield). Their research and conclusions can be read online at www.pilsburycastle.org.uk

PINFOLDS

The word pinfold originates from the Old English pundfald, meaning an animal pound or fold. Even into the past century, stray sheep and cattle were impounded in these small, stone-walled enclosures to await reclamation by the owner upon payment of a fine to the pinner, the man in charge.

Youlgrave, Birchover and Chelmorton pinfolds were conveniently sited on their main streets; Matlock had a pinfold at the side of Causeway Lane and that of Hartington stood in The Dale. Some pinfolds were located on the outskirts of their various villages, as at Tansley, distinguishable today as the neat oblong garden of Pinfold Cottage on Thatchers Lane.

Biggin pinfold stands in good repair beside the road to Hartington. Others can be found at Milltown near Ashover, Curbar (pictured), Cromford, Hathersage, Eyam Woodlands, Hope, Castleton, Monyash and opposite Hocker Farm near Longnor. Tumbledown entrances and walls are all that remain of abandoned pinfolds in such quiet corners as Bubnell and Bent Lane at Darley.

PLAGUE GRAVES

In 1665/6, the village of Eyam endured the worst outbreak of plague known to the Peak, although this was not the only place to suffer. Yet parish registers giving plague as the cause of death can be misleading: diseases such as smallpox and measles

may have been closer to the truth. Where true bubonic plague did strike, it was common for victims to be buried at the hands of relatives on unconsecrated ground. Such is the story behind both the Morton graves near the Barrel Inn at Bretton and the Riley graves at Eyam (pictured). Here lie the remains of farmer Hancock and his six children, buried single-handedly by their wife and mother, Elizabeth, over an eight-day period in August 1666. Miraculously, Elizabeth Hancock survived.

Walkers following a path below Baslow Edge may come across a sad cluster of burial slabs lying flat on the ground. Each is carved with the initials of one of the Cundy family from nearby Grislowfields Farm. They died within days of one another when the plague struck Curbar in 1632: Thomas

Cundy, his wife Ada and their children Olive, Nellie and Thomas. The sites of other plague graves at Curbar are now forgotten and unmarked.

POLES ON THE SKYLINE

In the days before signposts, travellers had only natural landmarks and stone guidestoops to help them on their way. Here in the Peak, tall wooden poles were sometimes set up on high, exposed tracks, visible from miles around to packhorse men and wayfarers. These beacon poles remained exposed even when the countryside lay under deep snow. One surviving example, Stanedge Pole on Stanage Edge (for some reason spelt differently) is set into a rock carved with dates going back to 1550, along with the initials of parish surveyors — wooden poles obviously need replacing from time to time.

The place-name Wooden Pole, near Longshaw, still centres on the lofty post shown here, at the junction of the Owler Bar and Foxhouse roads, where three old bridleways come together. The Totley Boundary of 1811 refers to this pole '... at the foot of which is a boundary stone of

this Manor with a T (for Totley) cut therein and date 1778; this we saw and made it more perfect by fresh cutting.' Local tradition has it that sheep rustlers were hanged from Wooden Pole. On a lighter note, a patriotic shepherd named William Gregory shinned up the pole on Mafeking Day in May 1890 and fixed a flag to the top.

Toad Pole field at Froggatt may be a corruption of T'owd pole, a now lost landmark which guided travellers towards a ford on the Derwent. A beacon pole on Black Knowl, described as rotten but still standing in the 1880s, gave name to Beeton Rod Farm at Stannington, pronounced Beacon within living memory. Early 19th century maps show a Beacon Rod on Longstone Edge. Other vanished guide poles include one on Dobb Edge at Baslow and Th' Stake, which stood at the head of Chapel Gate on the Edale/Chapel en le Frith bridleway.

POSTBOXES & PILLARBOXES

The first pillar boxes in the British Isles were erected on Jersey in 1852. Wall boxes were introduced five years later as a cheaper alternative, especially in country areas. Only the red metal door is on show, the wooden body being built into the wall. Surviving Victorian wall boxes are found at Cressbrook and Matlock Green. Cast-iron 'lamp boxes' came into general use around 1897, mounted on lamp posts and later on telegraph poles; an ER box is supported by a telegraph pole in Bonsall Dale. Again, this type is mainly found in rural areas where a small box is adequate.

Postbox and pillarbox-spotting enthusiasts come to photograph rare examples around the Peak. Buxton is high on their list, with its handsome Victorian hexagonal box opposite the Opera House. Erected in 1867 and still in use, it is known as a Penfold after its designer, J.W. Penfold. A similar version survives at Hartington. A wall box outside Heage post office is a great rarity. It is one of a small number which rather jumped the gun in displaying the cipher of Edward VIII, who reigned briefly in 1936 but famously abdicated and was never crowned.

QUAKER CONNECTIONS

Since its beginnings in the mid-17th century, the Society of Friends, familiarly known as Quakers, has had strong connections with the Midlands. Indeed, it was at Derby that George Fox, on trial for blasphemy in 1650, advised the judge that he should 'tremble at the word of the Lord', earning in return the nickname of Quaker for himself and his followers.

Quakers suffered years of intimidation, from rough local disapproval to imprisonment. One spirited woman named Jane Stones was condemned by the Justices to be stripped naked to the waist, tied to a cart's tail and publicly whipped at Wirksworth market. Four Quakers were locked in the stocks at Ashbourne; a larger group was beaten and stoned at Peak Forest; and a Quaker meeting at Eyam was broken up by a party of soldiers using extreme violence.

One Ash Grange, home to the Bowman family of Monyash, was an important Quaker meeting house over several generations; pictured here is the typically simple Quaker burial ground at Monyash. Followers in the Ashover area used to meet in farms at Buntingfield and Peasonhurst; the latter has a small Quaker graveyard. Denied burial in consecrated ground, Quakers also had cemeteries at Higham, Tupton, and Slackhall in the High Peak.

Today, the village of Fritchley is central to an active body of Quakers and the Friends Meeting House in Bakewell is also in regular use. Bakewell Old House Museum features the unique Bowman Room, furnished with family memorabilia and documents relating to their Quaker faith.

QUARRYING

In return for giving up our natural wealth to the quarrying industries, the Peak pays the price of an often deeply scarred landscape, a factor that excludes Matlock, Wirksworth and Buxton from the boundaries of the Peak District National Park. Our quarries played a major role in the Industrial Revolution, supplying stone for railway construction, iron and steel manufacture and for building grand civic buildings both at home and overseas. London's famous Regent Street is paved with Peak gritstone.

Gritstone extraction has declined in modern times in favour of limestone, often controversial for its impact on the landscape, while supplying the raw material for essentials from toothpaste to motorway construction. Meanwhile, disused stone quarries blend into the landscape and appear almost to have been created by nature, their dark and weathered rockfaces supporting an important variety of plant species and wildlife.

QUEEN MARY'S BOWER

Much of the troubled life of Mary, Queen of Scots, was spent in one or other of the great houses owned by her custodian the Earl of Shrewsbury, husband to Bess of Hardwick. The royal status of the captive queen assured her of considerable privileges, except that she begged repeatedly for more outdoor freedom. During her five spells at Chatsworth — which Queen Elizabeth was assured was 'a very mete hous, having no town or resort where any ambushes might

lye' — Mary enjoyed unaccustomed liberty, spending many hours in the walled and moated raised garden which became known as Queen Mary's Bower.

Writing in *The Estate – A View from Chatsworth*, the Duchess of Devonshire explains that the raised enclosure was built on the site of an ancient earthwork and adds: 'The building itself was largely restored by Wyatville in 1823-4 but its old bones are plainly visible in the thick walls and broad flight of steps over the moat ... There is nothing inside, and primroses grow on its flat top.' Its moat, now dry, is thought to be the last remaining fishpond of Bess's day.

QUIET LANES

Distinctive 'Quiet Lane' signs stand at either side of Conksbury Bridge and on Moor Lane in Youlgrave. They were erected in 2003 as the pilot stage of an initiative by the Countryside Agency for establishing a countrywide network of peaceful rural lanes, signed up to remind motorists to be extra vigilant for the safety of walkers, cyclists and horse riders sharing the same route. Surveys revealed that over three million people cycle every week and around five million enjoy cross-country walking, yet 65% of users feel threatened by traffic 'all or some of the time'.

Quiet Lanes already enjoyed moderate levels of low speed traffic before being designated. Wider plans for the future include linking rights of way networks, open spaces and places of interest; environmental protection and enhancement of country lanes; and steps to encourage motorised traffic to slow down to appropriate speeds.

QUIET WOMEN

A grizzly murder is one of several good yarns behind the naming of the Quiet Woman pub at Earl Sterndale. The most imaginative story has it that a former landlord chopped off the head of his garrulous wife when he could no longer stand her nagging. The inn sign has shown a headless woman since time out of mind.

Strange to tell, a more sinister hostelry of the same name was once in business beside Flash Lane on the desolate moors above Darley Dale. Its infamous landlady was in the habit of robbing and murdering her guests then burying them beneath the cellar floor. She was eventually hanged for her crimes but thereafter it was impossible to put the old inn to any peaceful use, for it was plagued by mysterious fires. One tale relates how it was razed to the ground just after a highway robbery which went wrong; the robber was in fact the landlord and he perished in the flames while hiding in the cellar from his pursuers. In the 1960s, a country club on the site was gutted by fire, as was a caravan subsequently used by the owner as temporary living accommodation.

Thankfully, the old legend has finally run its course and the property remains in happy and peaceful occupation.

QUOINS

This word may not be in everyday use but quoins certainly are. On a busy day, hundreds of pedestrians take advantage of this type of triangular refuge while crossing the old Wye bridge in Bakewell. First recorded in the 13th century, Bakewell bridge has possibly the earliest origins in Derbyshire. In times past, its quoins would have sheltered smartly dressed gentlemen and long-skirted ladies, all anxious to avoid the splashes and stones kicked up by horse-drawn coaches and carts. Heavy wear on the stepped entrances bears evidence of their usefulness. Quoins also feature on the ancient Holme packhorse bridge, upriver at Milford.

The River Derwent flows beneath old quoined bridges in such peaceful settings as Froggatt and Baslow *(pictured)*, en route for yet another example, this the narrow humpbacked bridge carrying traffic in and out of Chatsworth Park. Several miles downstream, quoins on the Derwent bridge at Matlock allow passers-by to step aside and enjoy views along the river and up to Riber Castle *(see Follies)*.

RINDLES

Pictured here is the unique Rindle Stone outside Grindon church. Its inscription, which has to be read sideways, reads: 'The Lord of the Manor of Grindon Established his right to this rindle at Stafford Assizes on March 17th 1862.'

Rindle is an Anglo-Saxon word for a gutter, in the sense of a brook that flows only in wet weather. A Tinkers Pit gutter is shown on a map of 1600 as 'a rindle coming to Dane' i.e. flowing into the River Dane. A short moorland rill to the west of Grinah Green, on the southern Ronksley

Moor, appears as Dry Rindle on a sketch map of 1933, described as nothing more than 'a thin tricklet in a shallow cloughlet'.

Romantic poets were far more familiar with rindles than we are today, hence this verse from *Hymn to Spring*
(Samuel Bamford 1788-1872):
'By dusky woodland side,
Silent thou rovest;
Where lonely rindles glide,
Unheard thou movest.'

And from *The Lily-Maid of Brindle*
(George Hull 1863-1933):
'Within a cot down yon hill-side,
Where a little brook doth rindle,
Dwells she that is to be my bride,
The lily-maid of Brindle.'

ROBIN HOOD

This legendary medieval outlaw has a busy role in Peakland tradition, indeed we are told that his companion Little John lies in Hathersage churchyard, to where Robin, or some say Little John himself, shot an arrow from over a mile away on Offerton Moor *(see Little John's Grave)*. The spot where the bow was drawn is marked by a stone post called Robin Hood's stoop.

Robin Hood's Cave is to be found on Stanage Edge and a Robin Hood's cross once stood below Bradwell Edge, its shaft now missing and the base built into a nearby wall. His name also marks a well near Longshaw Lodge, along with a spring, croft and moss on the Howden moors. Tradition tells us that Robin Hood's Picking Rods, a pair of gritstone pillars south-west of Glossop, were used to bend archers' bows for stringing.

A very tall story gives name to the rocky outcrop of Robin Hood's Stride near Birchover, pictured here. Legend has it that here the outlaw took a single stride from one pillar to the other, some 70 ft away. Both Robin Hood near Baslow and Robin Hood near Whatstandwell are entire hamlets; the former has an inn named after our folk hero, with an appropriate hanging sign in Lincoln green.

ROCK ART

In the late spring of 2000, a number of large gritstone boulders were dug out of the ground during levelling work at Ashover Primary School. After one particular rock was turned over prior to resiting, a member of staff happened to notice a strange sequence of hollows and circles on its surface. Then another stone revealed a shape and small hollow. The teacher realised that something remarkable had come to light, for the carvings reminded her of patterns which she and her pupils had recently been shown on a boulder at Gardom's Edge *(pictured)*. Those carvings were prehistoric 'cup and ring' markings.

'Cup and ring' decoration describes circular depressions surrounded by rings, some arranged concentrically, formed by using stone tools to hammer and pick at the rock. The Gardom's Edge stone was under examination by archaeologists working on The Rock Art project, headed by the Peak National Park and the University of Sheffield. The rock art tradition spanned more than a thousand years in Britain, probably beginning during the Neolithic period, with 'cup and ring' being the most common motifs. The Ashover rock art is possibly the most southerly example discovered in the country to date.

ROMAN BATHS

A neat, single-storey building at Stoney Middleton goes by the name of the Roman Baths. An information board admits that 'nobody can truthfully claim that the Romans did bathe at Stoney Middleton, but there have been Roman finds in the area' ... and there was certainly a Roman presence at both Brough and Buxton *(see Spas)*. Visitors to Stoney Middleton bathhouse can also read that 'The spring which flows through the twin bathhouse has a constant temperature of 63 deg.F and the waters used to be sought for the relief of rheumatism and such maladies as "too great heat" and "saltness of blood"! By 1815, there were separate baths for men and women, each with its own changing room and fireplace.'

The bathhouse was restored between 1985/92 and the spring that feeds the sunken baths is always decorated during Stoney Middleton well dressings.

ROPEWORKS

Many villages used to have a resident ropemaker and some still retain evidence of their long outdoor ropewalks — the work involved a great deal of striding backwards and forwards. A narrow, dilapidated enclosure at Uppertown, Bonsall, is where John Loxley spun hemp rope in the 1800s. A ropewalk at Winster is identifiable in the shape of a field, far longer than it is wide, facing the old ore house *(qv)* at the top of Bonsall Lane.

The vast entrance to Peak Cavern at Castleton housed a commune of ropemakers for over five centuries; their cottages, stables, shops and an inn were built inside the sunless cavern mouth. Early 18th century engravings depict housing which remained in occupation for the next hundred years or so, rent-free. Two rows of cottages 'built of stone or clay ... and thatched like little styes' stood against the walls and the soot from their chimneys can still be seen on the cavern roof.

The bedrock stretching away into the darkness is cut with a flight of level terraces. Each provided a ropewalk for one of the families or 'firms' who worked here. Their output included ropes for industry and shipping, bell and tow ropes, window sashes and occasionally a hangman's noose. Castleton brides were presented with a Peak Cavern clothes line into the 1900s. Rope making now continues as a

visitor attraction, against the eerie background of antiquated equipment under a massive, gloomy arch of record-breaking proportions.

ROWTOR ROCKS

This mass of gritstone tors at Birchover was explained to Victorian sightseers as an ancient Druid stronghold. Tool marks and socket holes certainly abound in the caves and tunnels weaving beneath flights of worn stone steps, some leading to roughly hewn armchairs.

This arduous sculpting was in truth the work of one man, local parson Thomas Eyre, who three centuries ago must have worked his fingers to the bone so that he could more easily climb up here to sit and gaze at the fine views now obscured by trees. Formerly known as Rooter, from 'roos', meaning to rock, the outcrop was famed for its rocking stones. Then in 1799, a gang of 14 youths deliberately dislodged a 50-ton rocking stone poised near the summit. Since that time, a 12 ft oval boulder which could be rocked with just a finger and thumb has also been immobilised, as has a pile of seven rocks formerly set in motion by pushing the one at the bottom.

ROYAL FOREST OF THE PEAK

Established as a royal hunting ground even before the Norman conquest, the Royal Forest of the Peak with its deer, wolves and boar was the jealously guarded preserve of the monarch. Almost 200 square miles in extent, the Forest encompassed as much moor and heath as it did woodland, the whole maintained and guarded by foresters, agisters, verderers and woodwards. Their gravestones, carved with emblems of office such as bugles, swords, arrows and axes, can be seen in churches including Wirksworth, Darley, Bakewell and Hope.

Bounded in the north by Glossop, the Royal Forest of the Peak extended eastwards to Derwent, Longdendale and Bradwell. Its southern boundary followed the Wye below Tideswell before winding north-westerly along the rivers Etherow and Goyt to Chapel en le Frith (frith is an Old English word for forest). The settlements of Peak Forest and Hope lay at its heart but its stronghold was Peveril Castle, where poachers could be accommodated behind bars. The castle grounds have traces of an imposing 13th century hall where the king, his retinue and nobles feasted on an abundance of forest game. Stones of an impressive hearth remain in place.

The Royal Forest of the Peak ceased to exist in the 17th century. Its deer were rounded up and slaughtered, leaving the land free for agriculture (*also see Vert and Venison*).

SANCTUARY KNOCKER

The south door of St Anne's Church in Baslow retains the base of a sanctuary knocker (*pictured*), the possible goal of fugitives and outlaws seeking refuge from the law in centuries past. Over a long period, anyone who committed a crime, even murder, could avoid capture by claiming sanctuary inside a church. There are no known records to say whether this took place at Baslow but the following Derbyshire reference appears in an Assize

Roll of 1269: 'William de Middleton placed himself in the church of Herthill [Harthill] and confessed himself a thief and received John Bolax and John (son of the Chaplain of Taddington) a robber, and abjured the kingdom before the coroner ... John Bolax and John son of the chaplain of Taddington are extraneous and outlawed.'

Sanctuary was famously claimed in Eyam church by Joseph Hunt, a 17th century rector who had undertaken a tipsy mock marriage with Miss Ferns, daughter of the landlord of the Miners' Arms. Unfortunately, his bishop did not see the joke and forced the couple to marry legally, at which Joseph's true fiancée sued for breach of promise. Litigation dragged on for years but the Hunts avoided redress by living in the vestry of Eyam church. This was where they spent the rest of their married life, where their children were born and where the couple were finally laid to rest.

SAXON RELICS

A number of Peakland churches contain Saxon stonework, carved at a time when our ancestors were embracing Christianity, between the 7th and 9th centuries. Dozens of stones with fascinating detail are preserved inside Bakewell All Saints' Church and its south porch. Wirksworth parish church contains an ancient sarcophagus slab described as the most remarkable in England for its profusion of early Christian images (see Wirksworth Sepulchral Stone).

Celtic, Scandinavian and Christian symbols appear on preaching crosses at least a thousand years old. The best preserved include those of Eyam, Bradbourne, Hope, Taddington and Bakewell. Plain by comparison is the restored Saxon font at Earl Sterndale; both church and font were victims of a 1941 air-raid.

A warrior's helmet excavated at Benty Grange in 1848 is considered to be the most important Saxon relic found in the Peak. Decorated in gold, silver and bronze, with a pagan boar crest as well as a silver cross, the helmet dates from around AD700 and is housed in Weston Park Museum at Sheffield. Buxton Museum displays a facsimile cross of pure beaten gold set with

a large garnet. Discovered in a barrow on Winster Moor, the original is held in the British Museum along with other Peakland finds including a hoard of 9th century coins, found with silver and gold jewellery at Beeston Tor in the Manifold Valley.

SCREWSTONE

This photograph shows a chunk of limestone containing what appears to be a mass of petrified nuts and bolts, some in cross-section. These are crinoids — fossilised marine organisms often called sea-lily stems but actually related to sea-urchins. The living organisms thrived on the edges of coral reefs during the Carboniferous period, 290-354 million years ago (see Volcanoes). The Natural History Museum website describes their preservation as 'the dissolution, by percolating groundwaters, of the calcite skeleton of the stem itself, leaving a sediment-filled axial hole. The width of this hole expands and contracts along the length of the stem ... The flanged structure resembles a screw' ... which goes to explain why crinoids were known to Peakland lead miners as screwstone.

Small fossil beds containing screwstone may be noticed in stiles and dry stone walls across the White Peak, whilst one spectacular mass is seen in situ inside the Fossil Cave of Treak Cliff Cavern at Castleton. Polished crinoidal limestone has been used in decorative work for hundreds of years, from fonts to fireplaces and from monuments to modern kitchen worktops.

SHEELA-NA-GIG

As the Celtic goddess of creation and fertility, Sheela-na-gig was always depicted in an unmistakably provocative pose. She can be seen in weathered stone carvings on outer walls at Haddon Hall, St Margaret's Chapel in Alderwasley *(pictured)* and St Helen's Church in Darley Dale. Although the detail is now weathered by time, it is still possible to identify the grotesquely lascivious hag who was credited with presenting herself as a mate to tribal chieftains, transforming herself into a beautiful woman at the last moment. One particularly impressive Sheela-na-Gig is carved onto a pillar in Melbourne church.

SHEEPWASHES

Sheep dipping was always a vital task on the country calendar because cleaner fleeces fetched higher prices. Generations of farmers would drive their sheep to a suitable stretch of the river from miles around, using a horse and float to transport any weaker animals. On arrival, the sheep were driven into a pen to await their turn. Farmhands stood waist-deep in the water to dunk each animal as it was tossed to him from the bank, though an observation of one busy scene around a hundred years ago tells how sheep were tethered to a sturdy pole and towed through the river by a brawny shepherd walking along the riverbank.

A restored stone sheep pen stands by Holme Bridge on the Wye in Bakewell but the most photographed sheepwash bridge in the Peak is a few miles upstream at Ashford in the Water. Here, the bridge parapet curves into a pen opening directly into the river, where the annual sheep washing still takes place in late spring.

SHRINES

At its simplest, a shrine is a place of prayer erected in honour of a saint. Two shrines stand a little over a mile apart in the northern Peak, separated by open moorland and the Errwood reservoir. Pictured here is the one built into a roadside wall near the Long Hill stretch of the A5002; it contains a

mosaic image of the Madonna and Child, with a shelf for votive candles and flowers. The second shrine is a tiny round chapel with a conical slab roof, hidden away above the ruins of Errwood Hall. This mansion was home to the Grimshawe family, who built the shrine in the 1890s in memory of their Spanish governess, Miss Dolores.

Older by far is a shrine in the Chapel of St Bertram at Ilam church. Bertram, reputedly the son of an 8th century Mercian king, renounced his royal birthright and spent the rest of his life in prayer and meditation after his wife and baby were killed by wolves in a nearby forest. Many people were converted to Christianity through his example and his tomb became a place of pilgrimage, with claims of many miraculous cures. The ancient stone tomb is generally covered with hand-written prayers on cards provided for the purpose.

SHUCKSTONE

Folklore offers two meanings for the word 'shuck' — either a robber/murderer or a phantom black dog otherwise known in the Peak as a boggart.

The Domesday Survey mentions a Shuckstonefield near Crich and there is still a Shuckstone Lane between Crich and Tansley. A public footpath from this lane heads towards the site of a former stone cross, of which only the hefty base remains. Its upper surface is carved with around a dozen weathered characters consisting of letters of the alphabet and strange unidentified symbols. Stranger still, this is an area where the so-called Beast of

Carsington has been seen in recent times. Even now, hardly a year goes by without reported sightings of some large, usually black, four-legged beast that is no sooner seen than gone.

SLICKENSIDES

Greatly feared by lead miners, especially in the Cromford Moor and Eyam Edge mines, slickensides — otherwise known as 'cracking whole' — was a dangerous natural phenomenon. It arose from earth movements rubbing together two close fitting galena-bearing vertical planes until they shone like mirrors. If a miner's pick struck a nearby vein, the sudden relief of stress within the slickensided rock caused it to explode and shatter with tremendous violence. This description of slickensides was written 150 years ago: 'The stroke is immediately succeeded by a crackling noise, accompanied with a sound not unlike the hum of a swarm of bees; shortly afterwards an explosion follows, so loud and appalling, that even the miners, though a hardy and daring race of men, turn pale and tremble at the shock.' The explosions could have a knock-on effect that continued for days — one occurrence in 1738 dislodged some 40 tons of rock.

SPAS

The geology of the Peak furnishes us with thermal springs, historically sought by the sick and infirm in search of relief. At 82 deg.F, the warm waters of Buxton even attracted the attention of the Romans, as attested by votive offerings now in Buxton Museum. In Tudor times, the town was host to a wealthy, aristocratic and even royal clientele. In the 1780s, with the only slightly warmer waters of Bath enjoying phenomenal success, Buxton Spa was similarly graced with an elegant Crescent, commissioned by the Duke of Devonshire.

In 1818, his aristocratic neighbour the Duke of Rutland built a bathhouse at Bakewell, but with waters at only 60 deg.F, its success barely improved on earlier attempts to move into the business around 1697. It was during this earlier period of spa revival that a large bathhouse was erected in Matlock Bath to make commercial use of the 68 deg.F springs, previously enjoyed only by the locals. This quiet, pretty village expanded into a fashionable health resort with the status of a spa town, all thanks to its warm mineral springs.

SQUINCH

A squinch is an architectural device built to cloak the transition from a squared or flat wall to a rounded section of masonry, perhaps a dome or spire. It can take the form of vaulting or corbeling, or appear as an arched spine built diagonally across the interior angle of two walls. The word 'squinch' is popularly defined as a cross between a squeeze and a pinch, but in truth it started out as 'scuncheon'. This word derives in turn from the Old French 'escoinson' meaning 'out of a corner or angle'.

Most British squinches are the prerogative of medieval buildings, and it is in the courtyard of Haddon Hall that visitors might marvel at this example, perhaps the only medieval squinch in the Peak.

STEPPING STONES

Overlooked by Bunster Hill in Staffordshire and Thorpe Cloud on the Derbyshire side, Dovedale is famous for a picturesque row of stepping stones that happen to link the two counties. Another fine set spans a wide stretch of the Derwent near Hathersage *(pictured)*, whilst a higgledy-piggledy chain of stones serves the purpose below Beeley, many miles down river.

THE STEPPING STONES, HATHERSAGE

Two series of stepping stones in Chee Dale are not there to carry ramblers across the Wye, but to enable them to skirt rock faces which drop right down to the water's edge, leaving no room for a footpath. The stones themselves are often submerged. Elsewhere, watery crossings might be just a scattering of slippery boulders strewn across remote moorland streams in places like Lumsdale, Pilsbury, Froggatt Wood and Padley Gorge.

STOCKS

Drawings in Anglo-Saxon manuscripts confirm that stocks were in use long before the 1351 Statute of Labourers, which stipulated that every English town should have a set of stocks for the confinement of its dishonest artisans. Twenty-five years later, Edward 111 reinforced the Act by ordering every village to erect stocks; public ridicule of petty lawbreakers and drunks was economical and easy to enforce.

The use of stocks has never been legally abolished. Examples in various states of preservation can be seen at Eyam, Uppertown near Birchover, Wormhill, Chapel en le Frith, Warslow, Little Longstone, Waterfall and Litton (pictured).

The oak stocks from Middleton by Youlgrave were removed to Thomas Bateman's Museum at Lomberdale Hall, their subsequent whereabouts unknown. According to a local publication of 1931, one of the stones from Youlgrave stocks 'is to be seen built into the wall by the gate where now live members of the old family of Rowland across the road from the churchyard wall.'

The stone supports of Hope stocks were built into the gateway of the church and those of Monyash are said to be incorporated into the base of the village cross. Chelmorton stocks stood in a croft on the north side of Common Lane but by the 1880s had been broken up and the stone reused in wall building. Into the 1930s, older residents of Matlock could remember a time when there were stocks near St Giles' church. On one occasion an old chap was found in the stocks by a friend, who asked what he was doing there:

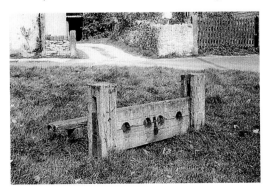

'Oh, I've only been clouting our Liz' ... 'Why man, they conna put thee in for wife clouting' ... 'Canna they? Abbut tha sees they has done. That licks thee!'

SUNDIALS

Until around 200 years ago, people in rural areas had to rely on simple sundials for time keeping. Communal sundials were often nothing more than a 'scratch dial' on the church wall, with a stick for the gnomon. As time went by, metal sundials were sometimes fixed onto old stone shafts standing in country churchyards. Winster parish records contain an account for setting up a complete sundial in 1721; the total cost of £1.9s.6d included four shillings' worth of lead for the figures on the dial-stone, with a further shilling spent on ale for the workers.

Fifty years later, an impressive sundial was installed on the south wall of Eyam church. It was made to the design of a scholarly clerk by a local stonemason who, along with the rest of the villagers, could hardly have appreciated its highly complex readings. The large square face gives not only the time of day and points of the compass but also the relative time in such distant parts as Jerusalem, Mecca and Mexico, not to mention the parallels of the sun's declination for every month of the year.

TARW TRIN

Almost forgotten now is an old legend surrounding a prehistoric burial mound 1,500 ft above sea-level on the summit of Chinley Churn, a steep-sided outlier of the Kinder Scout massif. Here, according to folklore, were laid to rest the bones or ashes of Tarw Trin, a Celtic chieftain known as The Bull of Conflict. Tarw Trin was given a hero's burial by his head-hunting warriors over 2,000 years ago. The 19th century historian William Bennett penned this rare reference to the cairn: 'He whose grave is on yonder cliff, his name was the foe of many; it is Tarw Trin (the Bull of Conflict) mercy be to him.' Perhaps the legend contains a grain of truth, for our hilltop tumuli may indeed be the last resting places of tribal chiefs.

TENTERHOOKS

The production and preparation of wool has woven a continuous thread through Peak history. Into the 1890s, the northerly village of Holme was one of the places to specialise in weaving woollen cloth. The village had a long, stone-built weaving shed, later converted into cottages. Still to be seen in a roadside wall between Holme and Digley Reservoir are about 20 large stones, each drilled with a pair of holes. The holes formerly held wooden 'tenterhooks', upon which woollen cloth was stretched into shape to dry. This process generally involved a large wooden frame called a tenter. The name of Tenterhill, west of Washgate Bridge on the Dove, suggests similar activity and a Tenter Yard Croft was recorded at Hathersage in 1657.

The wooden pegs at Holme may have slowly rotted away but the word 'tenterhooks' remains, metaphorically, familiar.

THIMBLE HALLS

The Peak has several Thimble Halls, all expectedly bijou rather than grand. Those at Hathersage and Matlock Green are in occupation, whilst the 18th century Thimble Hall in Youlgrave *(pictured)* has a new life ahead. It was originally a one-up, one-down cottage with a ladder for a staircase; no bathroom or kitchen nor even running water. Said to have been home to a family of eight around a hundred years ago, it was last occupied as a dwelling in the early 1930s by a brother and sister known as Charlie and Jinnie Frisky — not their real surname. Within living memory the tiny building has been used as an antique shop and a cobblers.

A Guinness World Records Certificate names Thimble Hall in Youlgrave as 'the world's smallest detached house' at 11 ft 10 in x 10 ft 3 in and 12 ft 2 in high. The property made national headlines in 1999 when sold at auction for an astonishing £39,500. Bids came in by telephone from Hong Kong, Athens and New York but even Uri Geller was outbid when the hammer fell to Frederick's of Chesterfield, ice cream manufacturers.

THREE SHIRES HEAD

This picturesque spot marks the tripartite junction of Derbyshire, Cheshire and Staffordshire, making it ideally placed in times past for various criminal activities. Counterfeit money was produced around the nearby village of Flash (hence, we are told, the expression 'flash money') and, to the great frustration of the authorities, illegal bare-knuckle boxing matches drew large crowds to this lonely place into the 1860s. If there was any danger of getting caught, offenders could simply step into an adjoining county to put themselves outside the jurisdiction of pursuing law-enforcers.

Wild 'button men' gypsies used to live rough on the surrounding moors. Their womenfolk dyed handmade oak buttons in the ochre stream flowing into the young River Dane, for husbands and sons to peddle around the countryside. Today the network of old paths and packhorse routes is trodden only by ramblers, so Three Shires Head has nothing left to hide.

TICKING GRAVE

This curiosity lies on private land at Hulme End. Its story is told in a Sheen village publication of 1984, the writer imagining a scene of some two centuries earlier: 'A little group of children in their long dresses or breeches, would gather around to listen quietly at a certain little stone enclosure opposite the old woodshop ... It was there that John Bonsall, a straw hat maker, was buried about the middle of the century – he had lived at the cottage (dated 1725) where descendants live today. He had been buried in his Sunday best – gold watch and all – and the story comes to us from this time that if you listen very quietly beside the enclosure, you can just hear the ticking of his watch!'

TIP'S MEMORIAL

In December 1953, 86-year-old Joseph Tagg perished after setting out for a walk on the Howden moors, where he had worked as a shepherd for half his life. His body lay undiscovered for 15 weeks in the deepening snow but he was never deserted by his sheepdog, Tip, who wore a track in walking round and round her dead master.

When Joseph's body was finally found, the dog was only just alive and she survived for barely a year. In February 1955, Tip was buried out on the moors. A memorial stone, paid for by public subscription and engraved with the story of her vigil, stands on the roadside above Derwent reservoir.

TITANIC TRAGEDIES

Amongst those left to mourn the sinking of the Titanic in 1912 was a Tideswell school teacher, Miss Ennis. One of the victims was her brother, Walter Ennis, aged 35, who had left a well paid position at a hydro in Southport to take up the post of Turkish Bath supervisor on the ill-fated liner.

Two members of an old Tissington family had also found work on the Titanic. Frank Richard Allsop was taken on as a saloon steward and his sister, whose married name was MacLaren, as a stewardess. She survived the disaster but Frank perished. Although his body was never recovered, his loss left the Peak with a tangible reminder of the tragedy, for his name was added to those of his father, James Allsop, and grandfather, Richard Allsop, on their headstone in Tissington churchyard. The

final inscription records that Frank Richard Allsop 'was drownded [sic] on the Titanic April 15th 1912 aged 43 years'. His epitaph ends with the words 'Nearer my God to Thee' — the hymn played by the ship's band as the liner went down.

TOLLS & TURNPIKES

With the introduction of turnpike trusts from 1706, road tolls were levied at tollbars or turnpikes, their keepers often housed in adjoining rent-free cottages. Many now converted tollbar cottages retain

Former occupants of neat cottages at Crowdecote and Leek Edge used to collect tolls from wagons taking chert to the North Staffordshire potteries, whilst a former toll house at Middleton by Wirksworth overlooks a route latterly busy with lorries carrying local stone. Wensley has an attractively converted toll cottage; built to serve the Nottingham/Newhaven turnpike, it was 'modernised' in 1760 with the addition of an oven and a two-seater Necessary House (privy).

Pictured here is the watchman's hut on the old Baslow bridge. Early records refer to complaints that this narrow bridge suffered constant damage from excessively heavy loads. As a result, it was ordered in 1500 that 'no one shall henceforth lead or carry any millstones over the bridge at Basselowe under pain of 6s 8d to the lord for every pair of millstones so carried'.

TRAMWAYS

A whole century separated the construction of the Peak Forest and Matlock tramways. The former was laid in 1795 between Bugsworth (now Buxworth) and Dove Holes to transport minerals and stone by means of horse-drawn trams. The system, which remained in use until 1915, is the subject of an exhibition at Bugsworth Basin.

It was a steep passenger tramway which operated on Matlock Bank between 1893 and 1927. Inspired by the San Francisco system, this was Derbyshire's first non-horse tramway and the first single-line cable tramway in Europe. Operating on an

a distinctive 'collection' window or doorway, as at Rowdale and Grindleford Bridge — this not far from another conversion at nearby Stoke. Rowsley has former toll cottages at either end of the village; that in Little Rowsley still constricts a narrow lane bringing the old Chesterfield turnpike down from Beeley Moor. Traffic passing through Stoney Middleton also swings past its old toll house (see *Octagonal Church and Chippy*).

average gradient of one in five-and-a-half — the steepest anywhere in the world at the time — the tramcars were drawn by a continuously moving underground cable, just over half a mile in length. A tram shelter from the Crown Square terminus, seen here, now stands in nearby Hall Leys Park, while its lettered glass window is on display at Crich Transport Village.

TROMPE L'OEIL

Translating from the French as 'deceives the eye', a trompe l'oeil is an object, generally shown in a painting, as so true to life that it is mistaken for the real thing. One skilfully executed trompe l'oeil certainly deceives the eye at Chatsworth, where a door in the music room is left open to allow visitors to admire a polished violin, complete with bow, hanging from a peg. It is difficult to accept that both instrument and peg are simply part of a two-dimensional painting, believed to be by Vandervaart. Some detail, including a pen, has been lost over the years due to what the Dowager Duchess of Devonshire calls 'assiduous dusting.'

There's a bit of a fiddle in the library too, where dummy leather books disguise two doors as bookshelves. Only their odd titles give the game away, along the lines of Cursory Remarks on Swearing, Boyle on Steam, Alien Corn by Dr School, or Jellies and Blancmanges by Somerset.

TUFA STONE

A geologist of the 1840s described the formation of tufa by explaining that certain warm springs had 'encrusted and enchained this incipient vegetation by the deposition of their calcareous matter to form tufa.' Put more simply, heavily mineralised thermal waters deposit lime onto moss, which itself decays to leave a spongey-looking stone behind. This in turn supports more moss to be petrified, so that tufa can 'grow' in banks up to 20 ft deep.

Tufa was sold in great quantities during the 19th century as the perfect ornamental stone for romantic Victorian grottoes, arbours and archways. It was quarried around Dunsley springs near Slaley and built the unique Tufa Cottage in the Via

Gellia. Vast amounts also occur at Matlock Bath, thanks to its many thermal springs. The village shows extensive use of tufa in lovely old mossy walls, rockeries, fountains and ponds.

TUMULI

The swirling contours of our limestone hills appear like fingerprints on the White Peak OS map, many showing a tumulus at their summit. The tumuli are the rock-hewn graves of our prehistoric predecessors, customarily buried with belongings for use in the afterlife. Most tumuli were used for several interments before being covered with a cairn of limestone rubble that would eventually become grassed over. There was probably a sacred significance in choosing such prominent heights as Chelmorton, Hurdlow, Taddington, Benty Grange and many others. An impressive number of Neolithic chambered tombs lie on the privately owned Minninglow Hill.

Around 70 Bronze Age tumuli are scattered on the gritstone of Stanton Moor, where excavations have confirmed that cremation was the common practice. Funereal ashes were interred in distinctive clay beakers, examples of which are displayed in Buxton Museum (see Nine Naughty Ladies and a Fiddler).

TURPIN'S TRACKS

The Peak is just one of many places to claim links with the notorious highwayman, Dick Turpin. In June 1737, fleeing north with a price on his head, Turpin carried out a robbery on Eggington Heath, relieving a young man of £4.14 shillings and his watch — but the watch and 14 shillings were handed back. The victim 'gave out that it was done by the noted Turpin.' The rogue was almost certainly familiar with the route through Longdendale (the present A628), a journey he made on his visits to Manchester races; a newspaper report places him at the races in August 1737. Tintwistle in Longdendale lays claim to the hammer and anvil that were used to reshoe his horse, Black Bess. The story goes that the village blacksmith, carrying out his task at the point of a pistol, was instructed to fit the shoes back to front to deceive any pursuers.

The old Chesterfield-Derby road is steeped in Turpin folklore and a map of the 1830s gives the place-name Turpins between Duffield and Milford. At Makeney his name lives on in a road, a meadow and a building known as Turpin's Barn. Into the past century, a Turpin's Post stood on Sadlergate in Derby. Roger Flindall provides rare references to Dick Turpin in *Mines, Quarries and Murders in the Peak District*. Flindall reveals how a burly Wensley farmer claimed to have been accosted by Turpin on Bonsall Moor but was strong enough to get the better of him. Furthermore, the pictured lead workings on Bonsall Leys bear the title of Turpin Mine, though this was not a local surname.

Dick Turpin was hanged at York on 7 April 1739.

UFOs

Inexplicable lights in the sky were known long before the Space Age. As early as 1716, a pedlar's news-sheet related how people prayed as never before when 'Great

Wonders of the Air' appeared over Hartington. Flurries of UFO sightings have been reported from all around the Peak in modern times, including the well-researched but inconclusive Ashbourne Event of 1980. It began at 2 am on 31 August when two groups of campers in Beresford Dale watched for ten minutes as light beams from a circular disc illuminated the sky. Next seen over Ashbourne, Chaddesden, Kniveton and Norbury, the object appeared above Biggin around 5 am and was last seen whirring above the Buxton to Newhaven road an hour before noon. UFO spotters were put on high alert nine days later when a bank manager and his wife saw two grey, cigar-shaped objects above Chatsworth Park.

On 27 November 1982, it was a 50 ft oval shape which distracted two motorists near Brassington, where a local builder and his wife had been woken around midnight by a dazzling, sweeping light outside their window. The light emanated from a 'cottage loaf'-shaped craft about to land in a nearby field. Once on the ground, during a stopover of about 45 minutes, its upper section opened to reveal to the shocked couple four figures silhouetted against a red glow from within the machine. No subsequent sightings are on record.

Strange sights were observed in the skies above Bonsall on the evening of 5 October 2000, culminating in an event filmed by a local woman after hearing eerie noises outside her home. She took several minutes of video footage and later gave a description to newspaper reporters: 'It resembled a giant disc with a bite taken out of the bottom. As it hovered over the woods, it seemed to expand and then get smaller again ... We could see it pulsing as if it started up and then it just went ... it came really close at one stage and I thought it was going to land in the field.'

The video recording appeared to show a large craft emitting red, yellow, orange and blue lights, with a dark circle at its centre. The craft hovered in the sky before moving to the right and emitting pulses of light. Finally it flipped over, displaying two scarlet lights, before disappearing in a red flash. Neither the meteorological office nor the military have been able to offer an explanation for the Bonsall UFO.

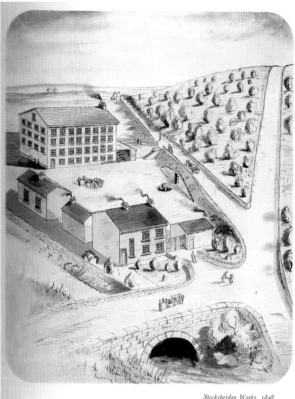

Stocksbridge Works, 1848

UMBRELLAS & CRINOLINES

Early umbrellas had fixed frames of either solid metal or flimsy canework, so a worldwide market was assured for the first truly collapsible umbrella. The story goes that the weather of his native Peakland hills spurred one man to come up with such a design. Born at Bradwell in 1815, Samuel Fox became apprenticed into the Hathersage wire trade and by the age of 30 owned his own wire drawing factory. This developed into the mighty Stocksbridge Steel Works, illustrated here in 1848.

Fox supervised experiments into the production of lightweight, ribbed frameworks of hollow wire, an immediately profitable invention thanks to the fashion of crinoline skirts and parasols. Of more lasting value, Fox has gone down in history as inventor of the world's first successful collapsible umbrella frame. Whilst this was indeed invented at Stocksbridge Works, and given the logo of a fox, recognition for

extensive work on the design should go to Joseph Hayward, a long-term employee and friend of Sammy Fox.

UNDERGROUND RICHES

A wealth of riches has been raised from beneath the Peak over the centuries: archaeological finds and fossils, oil, copper, silver, minerals and lead ore by the ton. Our most abundant natural resource, stone, has fostered industries great and small. Coloured varieties provided the lovely inlay workmanship of Ashford Marble *(qv)*; from Nettler Dale in Sheldon came rosewood, which produced the effect of grained wood when polished; Wetton and Sheldon provided bird's eye — a fossil-bearing rock cut to present cross-sections of crinoids so as to show tiny circlets; from Monyash came a mottled and veined limestone, varying in tint from faint blue to azure-purple. Different shades of barytes occur at Arbor Low, Bradwell and Castleton, along with the lovely Blue John stone *(qv)*.

URN MEMORIAL

Thomas Bateman was one of the most prolific archaeologists of the 19th century, a so-called 'barrow digger' who excavated numerous prehistoric burial sites around the Peak. His finds were housed in a museum at his home, Lomberdale Hall in Middleton, near Youlgrave. At his death in 1861, aged only 39, Thomas Bateman was buried not in a churchyard but in the corner of a field at Middleton, as he had wished. His tomb is surmounted by a replica of a Bronze Age collared urn, similar to those unearthed during his excavations.

His wife, Sarah, was laid to rest beside him five years later. Their tree-shaded grave is reached from a sign-posted path next to a former chapel on the Youlgrave road out of Middleton. Visitors will generally find a few wild flowers, leaves or even a potted plant inside the stone urn.

VALPORAISO

How is it that a quiet corner of the Peak shares its name with a port in Latin America? This came about many years ago, when a well-travelled man of Youlgrave made a favourable comparison between the lovingly tended, terraced gardens below Bankside in Bradford Dale, with the famously colourful hanging gardens at Valporaiso in Central Chile. Youlgrave accepted the compliment and adopted the name, generally shortened to Valpo. The gardens of Valpo are less formally cultivated nowadays, making them a haven for wildlife and plants. When the vegetation dies down in winter, traces of the old stone terraces, once bright with trailing flowers, can be seen from the opposite bank of the river, accessed from the clapper bridge at the bottom of Holywell Lane.

VERT & VENISON

This term was applied to offences against the verdure (vert) and wild animals of the Royal Forest of the Peak *(qv)*. Severe

poaching laws were introduced in Norman times and administered at courts held in the Peak; Peveril Castle was the major stronghold *(qv)*. During the reign of William the Conqueror, anyone caught killing hart, hind, boar or wolf was likely to be punished by blinding. Under the often brutal William Rufus, poachers lost no more than a limb. Henry 11 demanded execution but his son, Richard the Lionheart, devised 'a torture too barbarous for description'.

The accompanying photograph was taken from the keep of Peveril Castle.

VIADUCT VIEWPOINT

Distance, and time, have lent enchantment to the view in Monsal Dale, whereas the railway viaduct over the River Wye was seen as desecration at its construction in 1861. It drew the ire of writer John Ruskin, who protested: 'There was a rocky valley between Buxton and Bakewell, once upon a time as divine as the Vale of Tempe; you might have seen the Gods there morning and evening ... You enterprised a railway through the valley — you blasted its rocks away, heaped thousands of tons of shale into its lovely stream ... and now every fool in Buxton can be at Bakewell in half an hour and every fool in Bakewell at Buxton.'

Today the trains are long gone and walkers take delight in views both towards and from the viaduct, now part of the Monsal Trail and a favourite subject of painters and photographers.

VIA GELLIA & VIYELLA

Towards the end of the 18th century, Philip Gell of Hopton Hall laid a toll road along the floor of this narrow wooded ravine, west of Cromford. He named it Via Gellia, the Latin translation of Gell's Road, and its main purpose was to carry ore from his lead mines to Cromford Canal. In the opposite direction, the Via Gellia continued north-west to Grangemill, then on to link with the Nottingham/Newhaven turnpike near Mouldridge Grange.

In spite of frequent rock falls onto the road from Ball Eye cliffs, the Via Gellia was a romantic attraction for Victorian trippers, trundling along in open horse-drawn carriages to admire its vast banks of tufa and moss, wild lilies-of-the valley, cascades, and the knobbly tufa-built cottage below Dunsley springs *(see Tufa Stone)*.

In 1890, a cotton mill in the Via Gellia was bought by William Hollins and Company. Four years later, Hollins contracted the name of his Via Gellia Mills to give the brand name Viyella — the soft, shrink-resistant fabric that took his company into textile history around the world.

VIATOR'S BRIDGE

Each year thousands of walkers cross this narrow, twin-arched packhorse bridge over the River Dove at Milldale — Derbyshire on one bank and Staffordshire on the other.

The name Viator's Bridge originated some 300 years ago when Isaac Walton, inspired by his beloved Dove, wrote *The Compleat Angler*. His close friend and fishing companion, Charles Cotton *(see Fishing Temples)*, provided additional material for the fifth edition, including an imagined conversation between an angler, Piscator, and a traveller, Viator. The latter was reluctant to cross such a narrow bridge, which in Cotton's day had no parapets to obstruct the frequent packhorse loads. Exclaimed Viator: 'What's here, a bridge? Do you travel in wheelbarrows in this country? ... 'tis not two fingers broad.'

VICTORIANA

In October 1832, the surrounding countryside was scoured for flowers to decorate Matlock Bath for the visit of 13-year-old Princess Victoria. She and her mother were guests of the Duke of Devonshire at Chatsworth, where the girl planted an oak tree during her stay.

Many Peak villages erected tributes to Victoria during her long reign as Queen. They include a coronation fountain at Rowsley and, in Matlock Bath, both the commanding Victoria Prospect Tower and Jubilee Bridge on the Derwent, built for her Golden Jubilee of 1887. Diamond Jubilee tributes extend to a relief of the ageing Queen in unmistakable profile on a building in Tideswell, while a contemporary clock-face on Baslow church has 'VICTORIA 1897' in place of numerical digits. The most personal link with Queen Victoria is a circlet of flowers preserved in Edensor Church for over 120 years *(see Everlasting Wreath)*.

VISION OF A PRINCE

The glorious era of Haddon Hall was at its height under the Tudors, and Prince Arthur, son of Henry V11 and heir to the throne, was a frequent guest. A persistent legend tells that during his final visit, in the summer of 1501, the spectral figure of a woman appeared to Arthur near an ancient cross at Hassop crossroads, where he had stopped to rest during a lone walk. The apparition foretold both early marriage and death for the 15-year-old prince, who was betrothed to Catherine of Aragon. On returning to Haddon, Arthur learned that he had unexpectedly been summoned back to London to prepare for a November wedding. Within months of the marriage he fell ill and died, his last words 'O, the vision of the cross at Haddon.' It was his younger brother who, as Henry V111, inherited the English throne and took the widowed Catherine as the first of his six wives.

An impressively carved stone cross in Bakewell churchyard is thought to have been brought here from Haddon crossroads.

VOLCANOES

The geology of the Peak District, not least the existence of limestone, owes a great deal to volcanic activity during the early Carboniferous period of around 350 million years ago. Limestone often contains the fossilised remains of organisms that lived in the shallow tropical lagoon covering much of the present-day Peak District.

Examples of small volcanic vents which erupted through the sea floor have been identified at Grangemill, Blakelow Hill and Ember Lane, Bonsall. The recently published *Bonsall – A Village and its History* describes the Bonsall Sill geological feature as 'a mass of dolerite rock formed by the volcanoes. This lava bed can be traced up High Street and out to Brightgate.'

Millers Dale is another important area for evidence of volcanic activity. An ancient lava flow front is identifiable in Litton Mill railway cutting, where an information board explains that the local volcanic rocks are mostly basaltic lavas and chemically altered volcanic ash. The pillow lava shown

here was formed when hot lava entered the sea and 'the inner liquid parts of the lava flow congealed under water into rounded blobs of solid lava called pillows.'

WAKES

Historically, the wake was a vigil or watch kept by parishioners on the eve of the feast of their patronal saint. From a simple commemorative service, the village wake evolved into several days of celebration; as early as 1203 Hartington was granted a three-day fair at the Feast of St Giles. Similarly, in 1250 Tideswell gained the right to hold a two-day fair at the Decollation of St John the Baptist.

Over the course of time, many Peakland villages began to incorporate well dressings *(qv)* into their wakes, whilst sideshows would be set up, streets and houses were decorated and schools and factories closed down for several days' holiday. By Georgian times the 'entertainments' included bear, bull or badger baiting *(see Bull Rings)*, cock fights and dog fights, bare-knuckle boxing, freak sideshows and as much ale as a body could afford. To the deep disapproval of local employers, their normally hardworking labourers ran up such large debts that families were barely solvent before the whole thing came round again.

WARREN STONE

At a hidden bend on the northern banks of the Wye, about two miles upstream of Ashford, flows the Hedess Spring. Its pure and slightly warm waters are the legendary tears of Hedessa, a gentle shepherdess who perished on this spot trying to defend her honour. She had been abducted by the giant Hulac Warren, an act which so outraged the old gods that they turned him into an island of stone in the middle of the river, where he will pay for his wickedness to the end of time.

WARTH-ON-THE-OTHER-SIDE-OF-THE-WATER

In 1722, in the interests of public safety, Parliament introduced strict controls on the siting of gunpowder mills. The first application to produce gunpowder in the Peak came from Thomas Williamson of Shallcross in the hamlet of Fernilee, in the valley of the River Goyt. Williamson applied 'to erect and have Mills or other Engines for making Gunpowder with proper Magazines and Offices to adjoin thereto ...' A licence was duly granted in December 1800 for a mill known as Geldee Warth, or Warth-on-

the-other-side-of-the-water. In compliance with the law, the buildings stood a comfortable distance from the parish church and not within 30 miles of any other such mill ... with good cause, for explosions at Fernilee averaged one a year during the late 1800s, involving some very gruesome fatalities.

Production ended in 1920. All traces of the old industry were obliterated at the impounding of Fernilee reservoir in 1937. This photograph of workers in their safety clothing is taken from The Gunpowder Mills of Fernilee by kind permission of author Joyce Winfield.

WATER POWER

There is scarcely a river or fast-flowing stream in the Peak which has not been put to work somewhere along its length at

some time. Water power enabled the manufacture of an enormous variety of goods, from spindles and bobbins to paper, paint, flax and even the notorious red tape.

Many early corn and sawmills were converted during the Industrial Revolution for spinning textiles. The famous Viyella cloth (see Via Gellia) came into being thanks to Bonsall brook, which also helped to power Richard Arkwright's cotton mill at Cromford. Arkwright's Cromford and Masson Mills (pictured) are both open to visitors. Caudwell's flour mill on the Wye at Rowsley can be seen in action; its unique roller-powered machinery has served four generations of millers.

Bakewell Old House Museum has fragments of Lumford Mill waterwheel, which at 25 ft diameter and 100 h.p. was one of the largest in the country at its installation in 1927.

WELL DRESSINGS

Water also has a strong presence in Peakland tradition. We have had good reason to appreciate our wells and springs, of such purity that those of Tissington are credited with protecting villagers from the Black Death which so devastated 14th century England. It may be that Tissington wells were decorated with flowers in thanksgiving, giving birth to the custom of well dressing in the Peak.

It is equally likely that the tradition has its origins in Celtic earth worship, with floral tributes being paid to water spirits. The Romans also regarded certain water sources as shrines, decorating them with greenery and blossoms and making votive offerings; a collection of Roman offerings is displayed at Buxton Museum.

Nowadays, newly-dressed wells receive a Christian blessing on this lovely tradition, maintained by many Peakland villages between spring and late summer.

WHITWORTH SHELL

In 1856, the Stancliffe Estate in Darley Dale was purchased by Sir Joseph Whitworth, grown wealthy through his worldwide reputation for producing machine tools of unsurpassed precision. His major successes

WINDY KNOLL

This rocky knoll near Mam Tor hides a broad cavern mouth, tucked beneath an overhang on its northern side. Now high and dry, tens of thousands of years ago this was a waterswallow, where animals stopped to drink on their seasonal migrations. They perished here in large numbers after getting trapped in the swampy mud, leaving their bones to give us a picture of the Dark Peak in Ice Age Britain.

In the 1870s, excavation of a 25 ft by 18 ft fissure, now back-filled as a result of quarrying, produced 6,800 bones, tusks and teeth of grizzly bear, bison, wolf, roe deer and reindeer, the largest number to be discovered in so small an area. This bison bone is in Castleton Information Centre; other Windy Knoll specimens are housed at Buxton Museum & Art Gallery.

Vertebrae of a Bison
Found in Windy Knoll Cave,
Castleton in the 1930's

included the standard screw and a measuring device accurate to one-millionth of an inch. Whitworth also conducted lengthy experiments on field artillery and produced a far superior rifle to the Enfield, which the British army had found unreliable during the Crimean War. He also developed the Whitworth cannon, a field gun capable of firing a shell up to 6 miles and able to penetrate 4.5 inch armour plate. His artillery found a ready market in France and from both opposing armies during the American Civil War.

On moving to Darley Dale, Whitworth had a number of stone houses built on Church Road and Green Lane, their gables topped with wooden replicas of the shells fired by his famous cannon. Over time, these wooden shells have rotted away, leaving the remnants of just one sad survivor on Church Road. Sir Joseph Whitworth died in 1887; his name lives on at Darley Dale in Whitworth Road, Whitworth Institute and the Whitworth Hospital.

WINNATS PASS

Living up to its old name of Windgates, this dramatic blustery gorge was formerly a main entrance to Castleton and lay on the vital salt route between Cheshire and Yorkshire. In 1758, Windgates became a section of the Manchester/Sheffield turnpike but that was also a year of shame for Castleton, when a gang of local lead miners robbed and murdered an eloping couple in the pass. The lovers were almost at their destination: the 'runaway weddings' church at Peak Forest. For two and a half centuries, travellers have spoken of haunting cries heard on the winds that howl through the gorge.

At the construction of a road below Mam Tor in 1811, Winnats Pass became grassed over. It reopened to light traffic in modern times when subsidence forced closure of the Mam Tor road.

WIRKSWORTH SEPULCHRAL STONE

Wirksworth parish church contains what has been described as 'England's most remarkable early Christian stone'. Unearthed from beneath the nave in 1820, the stone is slightly coped and measures approximately 5 ft by 3 ft. The surface is carved in such profusion that the slab is

thought to have been the sarcophagus cover of an important priest, or even a saint. Confirmation of its very early date lies in the carving of the Lamb on the Cross, for a 7th-century decree ordered that this symbolic image was to be superseded by a figure of the Saviour. Two rows of scenes from the life of Christ fill the stone from corner to corner, barely touched by time due to the long years it lay face down under the church floor.

WISHING STONE

A guidebook of the 1890s assured the visitor to Matlock that the neighbourhood offered many points of interest where one could escape 'the incursions of the profanum vulgus'. One such was a large solitary rock known as the Wishing Stone, high above Lumsdale. It was especially popular with romantic Victorians, who came to walk around it three times in the hope of being granted a wish. Whether or not anyone now makes these circuits of the Wishing Stone, it remains a favoured viewpoint for people in the know and is still undiscovered by 'the common herd'.

X MARKS THE CROSS

An X may be used on maps to mark the site of a cross. Here in the Peak, Edale Cross served as a boundary stone or guidepost, whereas the 15th century Wheston Cross on the Wheston/Tideswell road — the medieval Crossgate — is a wayside cross, where travellers could offer prayers for a safe journey. Eccles Cross, its stump preserved in Hope churchyard, formerly stood on a track leading to the church, whilst Hope Cross is actually a moorland guidepost. Earliest of all are our Saxon preaching crosses. Sharing Biblical carvings with earlier Celtic design, they comfortably pre-date the churches where they now stand, including Bradbourne, Hope, Eyam, Taddington and Bakewell.

Hints of long-forgotten market days are recalled in a picturesque, stepped cross at Bonsall, a weathered old shaft at Monyash and perhaps the Butter Cross in King Sterndale. Knowsley Cross at Sheen is popularly believed to commemorate the 9th century Mercian battle of Longnor, while a similar tradition attaches to a stone shaft beside the River Manifold at Ilam. The far more elaborate edifice seen here, and clearly inspired by the 13th century Eleanor Crosses, was erected at Ilam in 1840 by Jesse Watts-Russell in memory of his wife.

Many crosses which disappeared long ago are recalled in place-names such as Hollins Cross, on the ancient track between Edale and Castleton church. Although any tangible cross is lost, thousands of feet have worn the track itself into a huge X.

XMAS GUISERS ·

In generations past, many Peaklanders enjoyed the Xmas tradition of mumming, or guising. The rhymes and mimes of these performances survived only by word of mouth and may have evolved from medieval Mystery or Miracle Plays, though with suggested heathen accounts of the Creation and animal sacrifice.

Families and neighbours gathered together when the boisterous and noisy guisers did their rounds. And into the houses and inns they tumbled: a bright and shining St George, Brave Bow Slash or Bold Slasher, a swarthy Turkish soldier with a name like Bulguyar, and a skilful doctor to patch them up after their traditional rowdy fight. Beelzebub himself appeared in most versions. Other common characters included the Black Prince of Paladine, The Fool, Hector and Little Devil Dout. Dressed in black and armed with a three-pronged fork and a broom, Little Devil Dout was

there to 'do out' (eject) anyone who refused to tip up a coin after the show.

The line-up usually included a hobby horse. Sometimes this was a real horse's skull fixed to a pole but in one village it was a magnificent beast with painted, rolling eyeballs, a skeletal grin of clicky teeth that clanged open and shut in a wire-operated jaw, and a hairy cover to hide four increasingly wobbly legs. It was the horse's fate to peg out and be resurrected at every port of call, so he had to be kept going at all costs, duly revived with mulled ale every time he (they) started to flag.

Guising had virtually died out by the beginning of the past century but one troupe still keeps the tradition alive in and around Winster. Their forerunners appear here outside Winster Hall around 1870.

X-RAYS

This common medical procedure has an important link to local mineral extraction. Certain types of X-ray require the patient to swallow a 'barium meal', and barium — which is opaque to X-rays — is produced from barytes, barium sulphate. Commonly cream in colour, this high density mineral has long associations with veins of lead and fluorite in limestone regions of the Peak. Lead miners knew barytes as caulk, oakstone or heavy spar. It was extracted from numerous mines including Ball Eye at Bonsall and mines on Bonsall Leys, Mogshaw Rake at Bakewell, Mawstone Mine at Youlgrave, the Golconda at Griff Grange and from mining areas centred on Wirksworth, Stoney Middleton, Castleton, Bradwell and Eyam.

Long before its ability to absorb radiation was recognised, barytes was used in industries including paper and paint manufacture. When pure, it contains nearly 60% barium. Today, barytes is produced in England only as a by-product of fluorspar extraction, with many thousands of tonnes processed annually in the Peak.

YATESTOOP MINE

This former lead mine at Winster holds a significant place in mining history, for it was here around 1717 that a Newcomen steam-powered pumping engine was first installed in a lead mine. The prototype had proved its worth a few years earlier in a Midlands coal mine. Such was the success of the Newcomen engine at Yatestoop that others were put to work around the Peak, their tremendous cost justified by greatly increased production. The installation of further steam pumping engines around Winster enabled the London Lead Company to reopen a number of disused veins where valuable lead deposits had lain waterlogged and inaccessible. By 1811, five Newcomen-type engines were keeping the Yatestoop workings open, a significant contribution to the output of Peakland lead and to local employment.

YEW TREE

Just about a century ago, a visitor to the famous yew in St Helen's churchyard, Darley Dale, wrote that the great tree was '... surrounded most wisely, considering the vandals with pocket knives who infest the roads — with spiked iron railings'. Protection would have seemed advisable for a tree then estimated at 2,000 years old, though modern-day analysis reduces that to a still venerable 1,000 years.

Its greatest girth seems to have been achieved at the beginning of the 19th century when, at 4 feet from the ground, the circumference of the trunk measured 34 feet 8 inches. When readings were taken in 1983, old age had apparently shrunk the circumference by 3 feet. Yet the occasional lost branch still continues to be replaced by dense young growth, attributed by late churchwarden Ernest Paulson, though not too seriously, to 'the excellent supply of nutrients from the churchyard!'

YORKSHIRE BRIDGE

Lovely as it is, the scenery of the Upper Derwent Valley is a 20th century deal with nature, her river and streams harnessed to provide drinking water for man, who in return impounded three large reservoirs — the Howden, Derwent and Ladybower. The final phase of dam building was completed in the mid-1940s, having necessitated the submersion of two villages, Ashopton and Derwent. Residents from the 'drowned villages' were rehoused in a new community of stone-built houses at Yorkshire Bridge, once an important river crossing on an old packhorse route connecting Derbyshire and Yorkshire.

YOULGRAVE FOUNTAIN

The private ownership of water supplies is nothing new in Youlgrave, where for 180 years the village has had one of Britain's few independent waterworks, and one unique to the Peak. It was through the enterprise of the local Friendly Society of Women, and local sweat and toil, that in the late 1820s water pipes were laid from Mawstone springs to The Fountain — a 9 ft high, 1,200 gallon collecting tank on the main village street.

Families had previously depended on local springs for their drinking water. On washdays, many housewives had to fetch buckets of water from the River Bradford, a steep climb home for most of them and the

hard water made barely a lather. With the opening of the circular, stone Fountain, households paid six pence a year for access to its single tap, unlocked at set times of day but otherwise under lock and key. In later years, water was piped to street taps and eventually into people's homes. In spite of modern-day problems with red tape, Youlgrave Waterworks is still bubbling along nicely.

YOULGRAVE, YOULGREAVE OR WHAT?

Depending on personal preference and the apparent whims of various authorities, here is a village with a record-breaking list of alternative spellings. Two versions remain in common use and residents have firm opinions as to which should prevail. Strangers, however, might be puzzled by a finger-post pointing to Youlgreave on one side and Youlgrave on the other. Road signs

show different spellings at either end of the village, while drivers leaving Newhaven are uniquely directed to Youlegreave.

The late Bill Shimwell compiled a register of nearly 50 different spellings of his home village, gathered over many years and dating back as far as 1086. The monks or clerics who compiled many early documents spelt names just as they were pronounced by the individual giving the information, so the list contains such

oddities as Hyolgrave, Oelgreve, Yolgreff, Iolegrave and Yograve. Youlgrave first appeared in 1492 and Youlgreave in 1595. Youlegreave, however, seems to be unique to the modern road sign referred to above.

ZERDATOLIA

This is one of several names applied to a Roman fort near Glossop. The site is now generally known as Melandra but even that came into use only in the 18th century. The Romans knew the fort as Ardotalia, a garrison built during their advance northwards around AD78 as an auxiliary fort to accommodate some 500 men. Protected by ditches and earthen banks with timber palisades, the five-acre site centred on a stone headquarters building and timber barracks. Traces of other timber buildings have been excavated outside the ramparts. Their presence is explained by Bill Bevan in *Ancient Peakland*: 'A small civilian village, known as a vicus, grew up outside nearly every major Roman fort ... Ardotalia had one of these villages. Here lived civilians who followed the army to provide services. Metalworkers, blacksmiths, shopkeepers, even prostitutes would all have lived in small, timber buildings ranged against the fort's defences.'

Buxton Museum displays a centurial stone which was probably built into one of the fort walls. It refers to work carried out by a 'century' of 80 men of the First Cohort of Frisiavones under their centurion Valerius Vitalis. The Frisiavones were recruited in northern Germany. The museum also has stone column bases from Melandra and an Imperial altar top found buried in the headquarters building. Zerdatolia/Ardotalia/Melandra was abandoned around AD140. There is public access to the site, shown as Melandra on the OS map.

ZERO — GROUND STATION

During the Second World War, with the very real fear of invasion and of the enemy reaching the Midlands, a specially trained covert civilian unit came into being to act as underground resistance. A top-secret radio transmitter, Ground Station Zero, was

installed in Tailor Toplis's workshop at 135 Smedley Street, Matlock. The arial was fixed out of sight on the chimney pot. A pistol, ammunition and hand grenade were kept beside the wireless set at all times.

Not a whisper of Ground Station Zero reached the unwitting neighbours until many years after the war, so it came a great surprise to local residents when Matlock Civic Association erected a blue plaque on the building in 1999. Worded 'GROUND STATION ZERO 1940-1944 Auxiliary Unit Wartime Wireless Station', the plaque can be seen left of the doorway on this photograph, taken for Images of Matlock & Matlock Bath by the present author.

ZIGZAGS

For ramblers and hikers, the best known zigzag in the Peak is probably Jacob's Ladder at Edale (*qv*), the alternative to a shorter but far steeper stretch of the Pennine Way. A wide selection of switchback roads open to motor traffic might include a lane that drops into

Crowdecote; the climb from Conksbury Bridge; a series of bends around Rake End and North Lodge en route for Buxton; and the acute corners negotiating the steep descent to Rowsley Bar.

Zigzags have also put the fun into funfairs. Over a hundred years ago, a riverside roller coaster was one of the attractions of Matlock Bath. The ride was advertised as The Longest in the Country, with a doctor's recommendation that half a dozen return trips would have a 'distinctly medical effect upon the LIVER.' On a good Bank Holiday, the switchback carried thousands of passengers and it was not unknown for proprietor Mr Buxton to carry home his takings in a wheelbarrow.

ZOOS & MENAGERIES

Riber Castle Wildlife Park at Matlock, often referred to as Riber Zoo, was one of the more enduring attractions of its kind. Established in 1963, the park built up a wide variety of native and European birds and animals. It was designated a Rare Breeds Survival Centre some years prior to its closure in October 2000.

A private zoological garden opened at Ashover in July 1955 as Pan's Garden. Designed to be run solely as a teaching medium open to visitors, this was the passionate enterprise of zoologist Clinton Keeling and his wife, Jill. A diverse family of animals was evacuated indoors in wintertime, until the family kitchen, as recalled by Jill in later years ' ... began to resemble a miniature jungle, containing a monkey, four squirrels, a hedgehog and countless birds of all shapes and sizes, as well as the family cats and dogs.' Outdoor residents included a bear, ostriches, reptiles, hyenas and agoutis. Overwhelming running costs forced the closure of Pan's Garden in 1971.

For several years from the late 1940s, a Mr & Mrs Pryor kept a menagerie of assorted animals at their home, Brookside in Calver. The large grounds contained three ponds that were home to birds including flamingos, black swans and toucans.

The Roaches in Staffordshire became a virtual wildlife park after a number of wallabies, a yak and a nilgai (Indian antelope) were either released or escaped from a private zoo around 1939. The animals had been assembled by Captain Henry Courtney Brocklehurst of Swythamley Hall, a former gamekeeper in the Sudan. The lone yak lived wild on the moors for at least 12 years, while the wallabies multiplied until they numbered around 50. Many died during the harsh winters of 1947 and 1963. Though often thought extinct, an occasional appearance has proved otherwise, with a sighting reported in 2007 by a family out walking along the Warslow road towards the Mermaid Inn: 'We saw a wallaby bounding across the road. It went into the rough ground towards the trig point. It was an orange-red, foxy colour with a black tip on its tail and black ears. I'm 100 per cent sure it was a wallaby. I've seen one before ...'

Shown here is Sir Philip Brocklehurst, brother of Captain H.C. Brocklehurst, with his pet monkey around 1930. (From *Around Rushton* by kind permission of Sheila Hine.)

The author has been writing local history features for the Peak Advertiser and other publications for over 30 years. She owes a debt of gratitude to the many Peaklanders who have shared so much information about this beautiful area, though it is impractical to name them all individually.

BIBLIOGRAPHY

De mirabilibus Pecci: Being the wonders of the Peak in Darby-shire, commonly called the Devils Arse of the Peak, Thomas Hobbes. Published by William Crook 1683

Tour thro' the whole island of Great Britain ... Daniel Defoe 1724-27

The Gem of the Peak, William Adam 1843

Lost Beauties of the English Language, Mackay 1874

Notes on the Churches of Derbyshire, J. Charles Cox 1875 etc.

Some account of Youlgreave, Middleton and Alport, Youlgreave Womens' Institute 1931

Sheffield Clarion Ramblers Handbooks 1930s/40s

Umbrella Frames 1848-1948, Stanley Moxon for the centenary of Samuel Fox & Company Ltd

Lead Mining in the Peak District, edited by Trevor D. Ford and J.H. Rieuwerts. Peak District Mines Historical Society 1968

Industrial Archaeology of the Peak District, Helen Harris. David & Charles 1971

Arkwright Society Local History Trails 1971 etc.

Peakland Roads and Trackways, A.E. Dodd & E.M. Dodd. Moorland Publishing 1974

The Story of Eyam Plague; Pinnacles of Peak History; A Peakland Portfolio, published by author Clarence Daniel 1977-83

Derbyshire Origins. Sheffield City Museums 1978

Stone Circles of the Peak, John Barnatt. Turnstone Books 1978

Stags & Serpents, John Pearson. Macmillan 1983 & 2002

St Luke's Church & Parish, Sheen, the Revd A.C.F. Nicholl 1984

The Estate – A View from Chatsworth, the Duchess of Devonshire. Macmillan 1990

Derbyshire Archaeological Journal 113, C.R. Hart & G.A. Makepeace 1993

Prehistoric Field Systems and the Vegetational Development of the Gritstone Uplands of the Peak District [ref. Leash Fen], D.J. Long. Unpublished PhD thesis, University of Keele 1994

Britain's First Inland Oilwell, Ivan Brentnall. Reprinted from the Ashfield Historian, Volume 13 No.3, 1995

Gunpowder Mills of Fernilee, published by author Joyce Winfield 1996

The Bugle, newsletter for Alport, Middleton & Youlgrave 1998 to present

A History of Derbyshire, Gladwyn Turbutt. Merton Priory Press 1999

The Land of the Etherow, Neville T. Sharpe. Churnet Valley Books 2000

More Curiosities of Derbyshire & The Peak District, Frank Rodgers. Derbyshire Countryside Ltd 2000

Stoney Middleton – A Working Village, funded by Peak Potential Millennium Awards 2002

Crosses of the Peak District, Neville T. Sharpe. Landmark Collector's Library 2002

The Spirit of Youlgrave & Alport, Bridget Ardley & Mary Bartlett. Landmark Collector's Library 2003

Calver, Curbar and Froggatt in Old Photographs, Brian Edwards. Northend 2004

Ecton Copper Mines, Lindsey Porter. Landmark Collector's Library 2004

Mines, Quarries and Murders in the Peak District, Roger Flindall. A special edition of Mining History, the Bulletin of the Peak

District Mines Historical Society, Volume 16 No.1, 2005

Bakewell The Ancient Capital of the Peak, Trevor Brighton. Halsgrove 2005

Around Rushton, compiled by Sheila Hine. Churnet Valley Books 2005

Bygone Industries of the Peak District; Journal of Natural History and Archaeology Volume 3, Julie Bunting. Wildtrack Publishing 2006

Bonsall – A Village and its History. The Bonsall History Project 2006

Around Longnor, compiled by Sheila Hine. Churnet Valley Books 2007

Ancient Peakland, Bill Bevan. Halsgrove 2007

The Bath at War, Charles Beresford. Country Books/Ashridge Press 2007

Wormhill, The History of a High Peak Village, Christopher Drewry. Country Books/Ashridge Press 2007

Under Grin Low – A Burbage History, David G. Owen. Published by author 2007

Early Newspapers and Local Records in Local Studies Department, County Hall, Matlock, Derbyshire